THE STORY OF A FUTURE ADULT

RUDI HEILAND

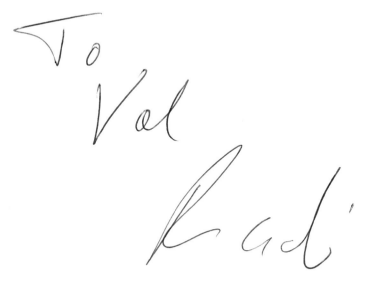

To
Val

Rudi

St. Neots
11 / Sept / 2021

THE STORY OF A FUTURE ADULT

Copyright © 2021 by Rudi Heiland

ISBN-13 9798534471694

ASIN: B09922F499

PROLOGUE

This is a story based on my life as a German boy born after the Second World War. Some information has been altered to protect the identity of others.

It is a journey through the highs and lows of life.

*

I have deliberated many times about how or what I could have changed in my life. What or who was it that shaped my life?

Was it the past that like a gargoyle jumped on my shoulder, not letting me forget the darkest side of humankind?

Was it my upbringing or my family?

I am searching for explanations, listening to the whispering excuses in my ears.

I became a restless and free spirit, circumnavigating obstacles when it suited me.

Maybe I could or should have done things differently?

However, the moral of the story is: There is nothing I can do about it now.

CHAPTER 1

A dream filled with nightmares of a childhood.

Only the dead have seen the end of the war

Plato

Actually, at the beginning I never wanted to be an adult because what I had seen, listened to, or felt so far did not fill me with enthusiasm or give me the smallest glimmer of hope. To be an adult was so far away, even further than the lost war, which thank God I had had the fortune to miss but my emotions lay heavy like a veil over all my daily thoughts.

Like an old shredded coat, which was impossible to throw away, my young and tender shoulders, were not able to discard this unwanted burden. It suffocated my words and thoughts. The lost and exhausting war had pushed human kind to the edges of reality but also had reminded them of the ground rules for their short existence.

In my eyes and thoughts, to be adult meant having grey hair, being frail and in decline and without hope for the future. All these adults with their deep, dead eyes could ever expect was a basic existence. With silent, screaming expressions, they were forming words and noises, which sounded like misery, loss, death and chaos. With jerking heads, they tried to find questions to ask any willing or unwilling strangers. However, nobody wanted to hear their questions because the answers were already obvious even before their pale lips had opened.

"Have you seen my husband?" The woman's words never left her, and remained anchored deeply in her mind, without ever being spoken.

She paused.

Her inner silence lay between her own question and answer.

"No?" She whispered.

She did not want to accept the answer, which she expected to hear. "His name is Guenther Mertens. No?"

She shook her head, like a sign of resignation; she tried to answer her own question. She was confused, not aware that nobody was there to listen. Regardless, she carried on, "he was in the 52nd army. The last I heard of him, he was injured on the retreat into East Prussia." The silence and a sense of loneliness seemed to engulf her.

"God have mercy on me," she whispered. Her hands tried to form the sign of the cross but she did not have the strength or belief to do so.

There was no answer, no reaction and no acknowledgment, only silence. God damned silence.

NOTHING! NOBODY?

Then, suddenly there was an emotionless and ghostly reply.

"I'm sorry," a voice tried to reach her through the surrounding devastation, but she was already on her way to carry on her futile search for an answer.

"God have Mercy," she whispered to herself again.

This shuffling wretch now hung her head deeper than before. Exhaustion and the wrinkles in her neck emphasised her physical deterioration. With her chin pressed deep into her ripped clothes, only her watery, fading eyes gave the impression of any fleeting emotion.

Suddenly, she heard the voice again, "Oh God, are you from Allenstein?"

As if, she was recognised, her breathing stopped.

"Did you know my wife? Gerda Nowak?"

She turned around to see a man with dark shadows around his eyes, wearing a dirty, torn military coat. His worn, lifeless hands appeared between the filthy, shredded sleeves, of this once so proudly worn uniform. His bowed figure had an air of resignation and despair.

"Please, maybe you have known her?" His shivering, pleading voice repeated the question.

She had no answer. To discover the unknown is impossible because who knows what death looks like.

His silence and painful reaction lingered in the air and poured down into the emptiness of reality. The tide had turned and she was on the receiving end of the questions. Her helplessness sent signals into his grey and broken human shell. "Oh God, no, not me, please do not ask. I don't want to hear it." These words resounded within her. Invisible hands covered her ears to block out any sound, as she could not offer an answer for the misdeeds of yesterday's world.

"We lived in the Masurenstrasse." His contorted mouth uttered a pitiful plea, "Number 36, please, please! I have not heard anything from her since our retreat. Her last letter to me said she wanted to flee with our children towards the West. She did not want to fall into the hands of the Russians. Her last sentence said she would rather kill herself and all our children."

He looked with pleading, despondent eyes, begging her for the slightest glimmer of hope. Tears rolled down the battle-hardened face of this ex-soldier. A man, who once sowed the seeds of death and misery during the conquest, was now reaping the harvest of that madness.

Silently, she prayed, "God have mercy on him!"

Thirty million broken bones! One hundred million broken souls!

Neither this soldier nor any other person knew what had happened to their families, at this moment in time. However, sometimes there is a small breathing space in the history of humankind, in which we can find an explanation for the past. Time can be a healer, but not for everyone.

The picture of this defeated nation is a mirror image of resignation, regrets and emptiness. Like a lost limb that lies in front of you, one realises with shocked incredulous eyes that this limb will never be part of your body again.

BANG, GONE, KAPUT, FINISHED!

The self-created past is now our inevitable present for a nation that followed his slogan, like a hypnotised flock of sheep.

Your leader orders – we follow him *(Führer befehl – wir folgen Dir)*

In one of his speeches he also prophesied, "Give me five years and you wouldn't recognise Germany again!" *(Gebt mir fünf Jahre Zeit und ihr werdet Deutschland nicht wieder erkennen.)*

The fucking bastard was right!

What did he have in mind for my childhood, my future, my life? Did I want to be part of his nightmare? I was not able to ask him, as he decided to leave us, on his way to eternal damnation. No thank you, I would rather keep sucking my thumb and postpone my entrance into adulthood.

But, hey, humankind knows this type of game. The stories of power, lust, greed and suffering reappear time and time again.

New dictators, tyrants and despots will fight for their own absolute power and consequently involve our civilisation in taking its place for another ride on this deadly roundabout. This madness is part of an endless cycle of purposely-created violence and no human being, so far, was able to find a peaceful solution to this horror.

This was now our frightening future.

CHAPTER 2

Where is God?

Who is searching for heaven on earth has slept during geography lessons

Stanislaw Jerzy Lec

Where and who is God? How will He judge us, on the colour of our skin or on the language in which we are trying to communicate with Him?

Is His decision based upon, in which invented man-made house we are praying?

Who will He save to go through the golden gates of heaven and who will He condemn to burn in the eternal fires of hell?

Will He notice the murderers and dictators, these lunatics, leading and condemning whole Nations to the abyss, at the final judgement day?

Will He punish these maniacs, who led millions of families to their death, and with a twisted ideology, robbed children of their lives, even before they began?

These questions may never be answered and the truth might never be revealed, but taken to our graves, until our planet, which we are so eager to destroy, disappears into a ball of fire.

Which almighty being allows such madness on earth? Is the image we are praying to, worthy of the title GOD that humanity has bestowed on Him?

Why, in His name did he send His son and let Him be crucified to try to save us? Was this death for nothing? Is humankind so desperate to destroy itself?

Has He forgotten His own commandment: "Thou shall not kill?" but let us go ahead with our own deadly destruction?

Who is He observing this type of insane game and watching our attempts to exterminate his most precious creation?

Maybe He never forgave us humans for murdering His only son.

Is God the Devil, or is the Devil God?

Who has the upper hand in this mysterious struggle? Who is directing us in our own struggle to distinguish between good and evil?

Even when His representatives on earth are objecting to this madness, why is He not listening or intervening?

Is the mist of our ignorance or belief in a religion a veil that prevents us from seeing the truth? Surely, people have asked these questions many times but has human kind ever learned from its mistakes?

These thoughts did not concern me as a child, as my life started in the present and not in the past. I was sure my God or one of his angels would protect and look after me and that my generation would reject this type of deprivation and disaster in the future.

My time that has not really started yet will have nothing to do with this devastating past, and our world will be a much better place. The sky will be blue and all the dark clouds of the past will be blown away for a brighter future. However, as I grew into an adult there would always be some doubts that would never leave me, expecting it could be a bumpy ride, but I was hopeful, we could still believe in the good of humanity.

Fingers crossed!

CHAPTER 3

My sister

The scars of our broken world are reminders of our past

R H H Heiland

If my sister Renate, had the same luck as me as a child, would she have had a different future? Maybe, but she was dealt the wrong cards, having been born eleven years before me. In that time, her generation moved into the abyss and had to survive the mental confusion of sleepless nights in this irreparable life that many took to their graves.

She was born in 1935 in the East Prussian town of Allenstein, which lay in the path of the victorious Soviet Army. During the retreat of the German Army, she was just nine years old and had to leave her home. What had happened to her was a living nightmare of unmentionable consequences.

She was playing alone in the road in front of the two-bedroom council flat that she shared with our grandma and our mother.

Father was away fighting somewhere in Africa. Many of her little friends had already left their homes, trying to flee to safety with their mummies and daddies, before the onslaughts of the advancing enemy.

Suddenly she heard the noise of approaching trucks of the retreating German Army. Then one of the trucks stopped and a soldier jumped out shouting, "What in God's name are you doing here?"

She tried to answer, "I, I....," was all she could mutter, with tears flowing down her cheeks. She was shocked and terrified.

"Are you alone?"

"No mummy and oma are in the flat." Her finger pointed to the window of the first floor. The soldier immediately took her by the hand and together they ran up the stairs.

"Hello, anyone at home?" his voice was desperate.

"Yes," answered mother.

"Jesus Christ! What are you all still doing here?" He was shaking his head with shock.

"You have to leave everything. You cannot take anything with you. There is no time." He explained in a voice that expressed pity, looking at this small, helpless young girl. Maybe he was thinking at this moment of his own children he had not seen for many years.

"The Russians are fifteen kilometres away from here. You must leave immediately; otherwise we cannot guarantee what will happen to you all." This was not a plea; it was a statement and a pressing demand.

With eyes wide open in shock her mother whispered "But we must …"

"Nothing, nothing, there is no time to pack. You must be out of here now if you want to save your family!" he repeated.

"Oh my God", grandma started praying in her East Prussian dialect. The realisation of the horror of what lay before them hit hard. "Mummy, where is my doll?" cried my sister in floods of tears.

Grandma withdrew into herself and whispered "God save us!" Then she tried to collect some sentimental items.

They realised with regret that they should have gone with their neighbours and friends who had already left. Leaving their home and everything they had known and worked for, was not an easy decision. There was no choice now. The alternative was death.

"Come now! Please, we have to leave quickly. I cannot keep the truck waiting any longer! All our lives are in great danger!"

Mother got her handbag, grandma carried some photos and my sister took her doll.

"Please take my daughter in your arms. I cannot carry her," it was the tearful cry of a mother. For the last time they ran down the stairs, not even looking back.

Then began a terrifying ordeal for our family, the officer lifted my sister first, then helped mother and oma into the army truck. They were sitting between injured and demoralised soldiers, riding into a mist of the unknown. Within a blink of an eyelid, dragged out of their home and the life they knew. My sister was crying in the arms of her mother, cradling her doll. There was no time or sense to analyse the situation, as everything was a blur. It was impossible to accept or grasp reality. Everything that made a home, the feeling of security and safety, was left behind and never to be seen again. Now they had only the clothes they were wearing and some meagre belongings, stuffed in handbags.

Grandma sat withdrawn, thinking of her two sons, Herbert and Allo who were fighting in Russia or wherever in this God forsaken war. Mother and oma's thoughts of pain and horror started to settle deep into their hearts and their brains were like over-filled sponges, unable to absorb the severity of what was happening.

FEAR, ANXIETY, WORRY, THE UNKNOWN, OR ANSWERS.

A long and difficult journey of over one thousand kilometers lay ahead towards the eventual safety of Lübeck, a town in the West of Germany. Even later, details of this escape were kept secret, as nobody wanted to talk about it, to relive this trauma.

It is unimaginable what my sister must have seen and experienced and what her little brain must have had to absorb, leaving an unrepairable imprint in her life, as death and destruction were her companions on this journey of terror. The consequences of this trauma manifested themselves deep in my sister's life. Sweat drenched nights, interrupted by screams or silent crying accompanied her for many years to come. It took nearly a lifetime to repair the mental damage she suffered.

Many years later, we learned that my father's dad, my grandfather, a very strong willed man, had refused to leave his home in Allenstein. They killed him, in front of his bakery shop, as he tried to stop Russian soldiers looting. A young soldier snuffed out the candle of another life with just one shot, executed without emotion, second thoughts or reason. Nobody ever knew what happened to his body. Maybe it had been thrown into a ditch or mass grave, as had happened to thousands of innocent people in East Prussia. He became an unknown statistic.

Humankind is capable of everything evil providing somebody teaches them. This act of barbaric behaviour was and always will be a part of humankind's endless struggle.

Why God installed this failing part in us, will never be answered or explained. Maybe He wanted to test his creation.

CHAPTER 4

Hope?

The hope is the rainbow above the cascading river of life

Friedrich Nietzsche

My name is Rudi, I was born in Lübeck in 1946.

My existence did not start very hopefully. I have no evidence of this beginning and I have to take the words of the adults around me at that time as proof. Shortly after birth, most of my skin, covered with a form of eczema, gave my body little chance to breathe. Apparently, my skin looked as if it had been burnt by fire. In the hospital, most of the doctors thought I would not survive. Only an intervention by a doctor who had studied under the famous surgeon, Professor Ferdinand Sauerbruch, saved my life.

(The first intervention of my guardian angel.)

My first three years I spent either in hospital or in a small two-roomed apartment with my father, mother, sister and grandmother, provided by a family that was ordered by the new German government to give accommodation to refugees from the East. Gradually I became aware of my existence and entered into the world around me. My brain started to tick and produced thoughts which I started to remember, even if I did not want to.

When I was three years old, we left Lübeck in the middle of winter, and found ourselves on a truck, chugging towards our new home in Hamburg. Our father had somehow obtained a job with the Hamburg Gas Board. I remember, apart from basic clothing, the only belonging we took with us of any value was a cast iron oven. We called it, "THE WITCH" because of the noise it made when fired. My father thought that we might be able to sell it later when cash was needed.

On each side of the truck were three wooden planks acting as a barriers. The vehicle had no seats, and was covered by a grey, smelly tarpaulin. The chipboard floor had oil patches and was very slippery. Many of us received bruises from falling across the floor during the trip. The ice-cold wind blew through our thin clothes and bit into our bones.

It was impossible to sleep or rest during this horrendous journey.

The tarpaulin was open at the back and gave us a view of the scenery that was to become our future. Our past was now disappearing at thirty kilometres an hour. We passed by people who were busy cleaning bricks which they carefully stacked, ready to build new homes, a new beginning. We saw houses with glassless windows and charcoaled frames, standing between the ruins of buildings, destroyed through precision bombing from our past enemies. It was possible to see a long distance afar, as no houses stood in the way obstructing the view. Only the remnants of walls standing, reminded us that there were once homes there. Trees, which bore fruit and leaves in the past, were now burnt and black.

As there was no window towards the driver's cabin, if somebody needed to stop for a toilet break, we could only communicate by knocking on the wall. As soon as I stood and opened my pants to pee, the ice-cold wind shocked me so much, I nearly forgot what I wanted to do.

The unknown irony was that the social housing estate we were heading to bore the name 'NEUE HEIMAT' *(New Homeland)*. I am sure that this choice was due to the art of the 'New German' management, as such a name inspired hope.

It started to snow and the flakes settled on the ground, partly camouflaging the destruction, and creating a feeling of inner peace and tranquillity. After the wind and snow had done their best to create a journey that I will never forget, I heard the carefully spoken words: "We are nearly there!"

I shouted "Where?"

Somebody said, "There, just look out!" Fingers were pointing, showing the direction. We tried to get up to see where our new lives would start but we hesitated as we realised our frozen bones were fragile. At the same moment as the truck made a sharp turn, my father stood up and fell back onto the floor, hitting his head on one of the wooden planks. Under normal circumstances, it would have been very funny. He did not move for a while.

When he came around, he cursed loudly. I looked at my sister and detected a small smile. That was the first piece of comedy for a long time and one of the first times, I had seen her smile.

My father was okay. He had survived years of war and this fall was nothing compared to what, had been thrown at him in the past.

Suddenly our parents became very quiet. Mother was the first to swallow hard. Painful gulps followed by a stream of tears. It was either a feeling of relief or apprehension. My grandma tried to stop the flowing tears with her apron, thinking of her two sons, killed in action and now buried with an unnamed cross, somewhere in the wilderness of Russia. My sister whom I thought was so big and grown up was biting her plaits of hair. Then we all cried without restraint. I did not understand why everyone was crying still I joined in. They realised we were at the end of a long journey that had cost many lives and taken away my sister's childhood, which would affect her for the rest of her adult life. My mother, father, sister, grandma and I were amongst the very few survivors, as other family members either had been killed, or were missing.

Then we saw a large building. A block of flats, a red brick monster was standing alone amongst the ruins and bomb craters. This gigantic building, four storeys high would become our new place of happiness and sorrow. It would accommodate hundreds of families who would be both friends and enemies, my mouth fell open and I was stunned. We had arrived at our home, our sanctuary in Hamburg Barmbek, where our new life would begin.

The whole building was cold and unfinished with concrete steps leading to the upper floors. The smell of the concrete created a nasty taste in my mouth. There were no railings on the stairs and very few lamps on the ceilings. Builders were working, sawing, hammering and carrying planks of wood and sacks of cement all needed to complete the work.

We were one of the first families to move in. Our flat was on the ground floor and was barren without any furniture. My parents took very few belongings with them so it did not take long to unpack. The only thing I remember were two old records by Zarah Leander and Richard Tauber. It is strange what your brain lets you remember. Only God knows why such irrelevant thoughts are stored in our brain. He works in mysterious ways.

Our ground floor flat was small. They called it compact. It consisted of a small hall, one miniature kitchen, and two bedrooms. One bedroom doubled up as a lounge. A coal-fired oven stood in the kitchen, providing us with warmth. The walls were all painted white. I am sure it must have felt like paradise to my parents and oma, after the uncertain years of fleeing and living off the mercy of others.

My parents quickly acquired some basic furniture and other essential utilities, on credit.

Our bathroom was narrow and contained a tall copper tank that was wood and coal fired and connected to a bathtub to supply us with warm water. Taking a bath was allowed only on selected weekends. There was a clear order of precedence in the use of this treasured facility. First father, then mother, next my sister and occasionally Grandma. Lastly, as the water started to change colour, it was my turn.

Grandma directed the household with authority, and a type of a chaotic order took hold. In the early days, my tiny body was often soaked in the water of a small zinc tub that stood on the floor in the lounge.

I was bathed sometimes in the kitchen sink. This white porcelain container was just big enough for me to squeeze in with hunched knees as long as any pots or pans were removed. Grandma took full control and she scrubbed every part of my tender body. Mainly using cold water, as the warm water had already been used to clean the crockery. Anyway, cold water makes you stronger was the motto. She used a scratching material which she called soap.

"Dear God, don't be such a wuss, a bit of scrubbing does not harm. It is good for your body and makes you harder," she let me know. "Stop whingeing. Oh dear, the youth of today!" she would complain.

She shook her head and lifted me out of the sink and my cold body disappeared into a large towel. After this treatment, I would sit in a chair sucking on my warm milk bottle.

At nighttime, father and mother used a dark blue, velvety looking convertible L-shaped sofa for their bed in the lounge, and slept on different sides. Their flames of sexual attraction extinguished long ago, and any feelings of tenderness or love were in the past. I had the suspicion and later the confirmation that my birth might have been the trigger, because I was unwanted by my father. He felt it was his wife's fault and that I inconvenienced his life; he therefore halted all passionate and sexual activities with her.

CHAPTER 5

Hello, I am here

I am more interested in the future than the past, because I consider living in it

Albert Einstein

Let us see what life has to offer. I was moving in a direction, of which I had no control. I hoped and prayed that things would be okay.

In the following years, some of the darkness of the past slowly disappeared into the mist of distant memories. People, from all walks of life moved in to the vacant flats. I made new friends. We invented games like Cowboys and Indians, and we even pretended to be soldiers. How feeble are a child's memories?

We explored the corridors of cellars that ran below the vast block of flats. There were individual rooms allocated to each flat in which potatoes were stored in self-made wooden boxes, next to sacks of coal. Signs of accumulated wealth, such as bicycles, scooters, cases and cartons of unwanted gifts, started to appear, announcing a new era.

With new hope developing in their hearts and minds, people proclaimed, 'Just wait, times will soon be better.' Many could feel the new established Deutsche Mark in the pockets of their new outfits, and were experiencing an atmosphere of security and normality. However, not everybody had the same good fortune to share this phenomenon.

We all kept our fingers and everything else crossed that we were on our way to a better future.

*

I was sitting on the cold damp floor of our flat with my legs stretched out and my hands supporting my head. My eyes darted around, making sure I would not miss anything. Feeling anxious but excited, I was waiting for what was going to happen next. I got up, pulling on my socks to go and look out of the window. A light rain was falling from the grey Hamburg sky. Just across our street, I could see an allotment with mishmash of shrubs and plants, which without any doubt, needed care and attention. I looked at the remains of walls and damaged concrete sheds. It was an area with hidden treasures, waiting to be explored. It became our preferred playground.

Hamburg could have been in the Guinness Book of Records for the largest man made playground in the world, as sixty percent of the city had been destroyed.

I went outside. There was a road with two pavements, one leading to our front door No 2. Nearby, they had installed black painted gas lanterns and their shimmering light felt like it protected us, radiating an atmosphere of peace at night.

In the middle of our street was an island of soil with a very big chestnut tree in the centre. It stood proud, covered in a glowing green, creating hope that its life would continue. I stood in front of this tree and thought that they must have built the block of flats carefully around this beautiful, symbol of hope. I was sure that in future it would shed its golden leaves and drop conkers on us children, happily playing below.

However, there were wagging, warning fingers, reminding us, that bombs had showered on Hamburg, which had decimated the ground, and created a carpet of unexploded devices, on top of which we now played.

My steps took me nearer to the fences of the allotment. This place became a sanctuary for many widowers, widows and returning prisoners of the lost war. They worked with shovels and hoes to grow food for their meagre tables and gave them a sense of purpose for their existence.

Between these sections of damaged society, I noticed an elderly man; his name was Herr Rabler, as I later found out. He was sitting on a wooden box behind his rusty fence. What

I noticed first were his eyes. They were different. They did not reflect the gloom and defeat that I had seen in many other people. I even detected a glimmer of hope in his face that was still marked by endless stories of his experiences. Anyhow, his face was friendly and approachable. I realised that the once so popular moustache of past years was gone and had now been replaced by a well-groomed beard. It did not take long for me to make friends with him and after some months, I became his helper.

Herr Rabler had started a small business and kept chickens. They ran around in a small coop and when demand for fresh meat was required, mainly on the weekend, he swung his axe and chopped the selected victim's heads off. After my initial shock at such events, I started to find it funny. I watched Herr Rabler catch one of the feathered food providers, and put it flat on a wooden block and with a 'smack,' the head would come off, and a ghostly spectacle would start. The head would fall into a bucket and the rest of the body would run like crazy in a circle then stop abruptly, as if somebody had suddenly put the brakes on, and the headless body would then keel over. Soon after that, feathers would fly through the air. I eventually became accustomed to these procedures and sometime later, as an acknowledgement of my completed apprenticeship in his business, he rewarded me with a freshly plucked chicken that I proudly presented to my mother. This was a welcome change to the usual nettle soup, spinach and other supplements, which helped to keep us healthy.

Actually, I never knew if I was of any help to Herr Rabler, maybe he just did not want to be alone. Maybe I showed him how to laugh again. A child without the baggage of the traumatic past can sometimes act as a healing cloth, covering an open wound and allow it to forget the pain.

*

At six years old, I was still sucking my thumb and every night put to bed with a bottle of warm milk. I just hoped that none of my friends would see me like this; otherwise, my reputation would not survive. My security blanket was never far from me. It was my bastion against any dark thoughts, which might be still lurking outside and trying to disturb me. A shield that would protect me against everything that wanted to hurt me.

My tender body was still covered with eczema, but I now felt ready to enjoy my life. My snow-white hair crowned a pale glass-like face. A monthly trip to a clinic was arranged, where I was made to lie on a sunbed for ten minutes to enrich my body with vitamin D.

The days passed by without any newsworthy events. We played marbles and other games with self-made equipment. We played hockey on the road with sticks and an empty tin for a ball. We would trick people by laying a purse on the sandy path, attached to a hidden string, and then wait behind the bushes for a victim to see it. The moment a passer-by bent down to grab the purse, we pulled the string and watched a very perplexed person look around, holding only a handful of sand.

I received kisses from mother, grandma, and the occasional clips around the ear from father. I started to learn how this family worked.

Then winter announced its arrival. The first snow fell and its white blanket filled me with happiness. I was comfortable in my little world. Christmas was nearly upon us. One morning I jumped out of bed and pressed my nose against the cold frozen window to view a white wonderland. My breath cleared some ice off the glass and the image of my smiling face appeared. Then I noticed somebody had stacked a large pile of Christmas trees against the rusty allotment fence. I ran into the kitchen, had a quick wash and put on my wellies and warm clothes. My bobble hat, which was always part of my outfit, crowned my head. It became a symbol of me and soon my friends would call out, "Here comes bobble hat".

I approached the seller and acted as if I were interested in his trees. After my pleading and suggestions of helping, the Christmas tree seller gained an assistant. My second apprenticeship had started. My new boss told me: "Listen carefully; the small trees cost two Mark and the larger ones we sell for five Mark. Is that clear?" "Jawohl, I understand!" I shouted.

I helped him with the selling and delivered many trees to our customer's flats. I was excited and could not wait for the next working day. The Christmas tree business flourished and pocket money enhanced my happiness. At the end of my commercial venture, I was presented with a tree for our family.

"Here my boy, you've done a good job. Now take this one to your mum and…. Thanks and MERRY CHRISTMAS". He shook my hand as if I was a grown-up.

When I presented this gift to my mum and grandma, I was praised and promoted to being the best child, just behind the birthday child, called Jesus. This filled me with internal warmth and for a fleeting moment, the world was perfect. Everything in the house started to smell good and felt good in anticipation of Christmas.

It was a German tradition that children were not allowed into 'THE ROOM' to see the decorated Christmas tree, until Christmas Eve. A little bell rang to call me into the room where a feeling of happiness touched me. God, His son with his stepparents Mary and Joseph were also guests in our council residence.

Real candles which father had bought on the black market decorated MY tree. On a previous occasion, our normal routine was interrupted when the police knocked on our door to report that father had been arrested for some black market activities. However, as he was only one of many, he was released with a caution, but his goods were confiscated. This, of course delayed our timetable to become rich.

We wished each other Merry Christmas and Peace on Earth. Then the inevitable and haunting silence struck me. The deeply embedded anxiety of the past had not left the family and the overwhelming memories of the dead, the missing and the lost homeland took hold. Grandma folded her hands and started praying. Her lips moved but only God could hear her. She then whispered, as if it was a question. "But they are all with us and within us." Tears filled her tired eyes and fell on her praying hands. She looked at us as if she was searching for confirmation and understanding. Mother's tearful eyes glimmered in the light. In her face, I saw the horror of the past she was fighting. Her cramped and tense hands tried to help her praying. Maybe it was her way of cleansing, escaping the past with its endless nightmares on tear soaked pillows. We glided through that moment of despair and silence.

Still, Christmas Eve was beautiful in my childish world. The magic of fairy tales, warmth and thoughts of redemption filled the room. I tried to remember and perform my compulsory poem and the real, flickering 'black market' candles created a homely atmosphere. I was encouraged to enhance the mood and started to use my dubious musical skills to play on the recorder, father had won at a card game in a pub. To save everybody's hearing, my performance was cut short with some muted applause.

Suddenly, there was a knock on the door. "Who can this be?" asked mother in a mischievous voice. She went and opened the door. "Oh, look who is here," she shouted.

I was shocked and covered my mouth with clasping hands. "Father Christmas!" I screamed and slid from my chair, with my legs trembling. Thoughts rushed through my head. I saw him some time ago in a shop. He did not acknowledge me then and now he is here, he comes to me? I was frightened, anguished but excited.

"Are you the little boy called Rudi?" he addressed me. "Have you always been well behaved?" he asked me, breathing heavily. I did not recognise him as the nice Father Christmas I had seen before. His voice was sharp and his eyes revealed no warmth, love, or understanding.

"Yes," I whispered.

I realised that Father Christmas was reeking of some substance and I did not understand why he was talking with a slurred voice.

"Hmm," he mumbled with a frown, "what about when your mother asked you to help her?" His piercing eyes, like poisonous darts, frightened me. I stood in front of him and swallowed hard. 'How does he know all this?' I asked myself.

I heard him saying. "So, because you have not obeyed your mother I have this broom for you." He took his sack from his shoulders and revealed a broom, for me to take. I was in a nightmare, as I experienced this, through the curtains of my now flowing tears.

"You promise me that you will behave from now on?" He continued.

I could not answer. I was paralysed!

"Stop crying". His mumbling words were difficult to understand.

"I also heard that you helped your mother many times, is that so?"

I could not talk, but only nodded my head and realised that I was still holding the broom. "Well, I don't think it is all that bad. Come here I have something else for you."

Slowly and carefully, I eased towards him. With his shaking hands, he gave me a small parcel. I wanted to grab it and run out of the room as quickly as possible.

"Well, what have you got to say to Father Christmas?" mother asked.

"Thank you." I said without conviction and moved quickly away. I opened my present and out of the colourful paper, a wooden locomotive with a red chimney and a green body appeared. I pushed it across the floor, and on my way, I hid the broom behind the Christmas tree.

The highlight of our Christmas dinner was another chicken Herr Rabler had given me. With this, I became the provider of the Christmas dinner's main ingredients. Unfortunately, even during this festive meal the hated spinach appeared, shoved onto my plate. I waited until all eyes were fixed on their own dinners or in father's case, on the drink, and then I scraped it off.

After dinner, it was traditional for us all to sit around and listen to the radio. One of the main programmes was called, 'Greetings from Sailors from all corners of the world to the loved ones at home.' It was a broadcast from ships travelling around the world. Sometime it was not easy to understand the seamen, as the sounds of their voices were distorted by the crackling and whistling of the airwaves.

During a quiet moment I was told, that Grandma did something after the First World War or before the Second World War (take your pick) which could only be described as the greatest deed of love. During that time, she lived as a very young mother with three small children in a small flat in Allenstein, East Prussia. Her husband never returned from the hellish battlefields of the Somme. She volunteered in an orphanage. One day, without any hesitation she adopted a baby.

"Why did you do this?" I asked. Tears started to appear, which hardly left her today.

"I felt sorry for him because I was sure nobody else would have adopted him. He was not the strongest and best looking child." She called him Günter and he became a brother to my sister. I only ever knew him as an adult, as he was much older. He was not living in our family home when I was young, because he became a merchant sailor and travelled the world. Now it started to make sense why we were all sitting around the radio on Christmas Eve and listening to this programme. Maybe we would hear his name read out.

When he was on leave and stayed with us, he told me the most exciting stories about the countries he had visited. For instance, when he was in Africa and made a trip on the Congo Express Railway or watched whales and sharks in South Africa. He had even danced at the famous carnival in Rio de Janeiro. I wished I could have been with him. It might be that his stories inspired my desire to travel the world.

Afterwards we sat around the Christmas tree and enjoyed the quietness and the peace of those special moments. Just as we got up mother said, "Oh, by the way there is something else for you but it is too late now so it will have to wait until tomorrow." I hardly slept that night.

CHAPTER 6

Father tried to be a father

"Mothers are fonder than fathers of their children because they are more certain they are their own"

Aristotle

After a nearly sleepless night, I awoke very early the next morning to start my search for the missing present. Washing my face and brushing my teeth had to wait. I was full of hope as I rummaged through the whole flat because mother had mentioned that there was something more for me. Her announcement sounded mysterious. I was over excited, but I found nothing.

Finally, after breakfast, mother asked my father, "Hans, have you got something else for the boy?"

"Hmm, yes, wait a minute I'll be straight back," he answered and wiped the traces of strawberry jam off his chin. He put on his slippers and disappeared into the cellar. After a short while, he came back into the kitchen and announced, "Go, have a look!" The way he said it, left only one conclusion; it had to be big, something special. I ran excitedly into the hallway. I could not believe my eyes. There were two pieces of wooden boards leaning against the wall.

"Well, do you like it?" His smirk gave away the idea that he was going to show me something unusual and was proud of it.

"What is THAT?" I asked with obvious puzzlement.

"Skis, you strap them on your feet and can glide through the snow and down hills," he replied.

Frustrated, I asked with a frown. "I can do what with them? I can move on these planks?"

He must have realised my disappointment, because something quite unusual happened. He offered to spend some time with me, to show me what to do. "Come on son get dressed we're going skiing." He laughed in such a good mood. I was curious, waiting for things to happen. The freshly fallen snowflakes reminded me to dress warmly.

"Ready?"

"Yep," I answered through my scarf and tried to hold his hand.

What a picture! Two warmly dressed figures walking through the snow, searching for a hill or at least a mound in the flattest part of Germany.

"Here, hold those ski sticks, you need them to start moving," he said, wedging the two wooden planks under his arm. I was just thinking what a good mood he was in when reality struck. It stared to snow very heavily and after some careful first steps, he lost his balance on the icy path. I saw the two skis flying through the air and fathers legs buckling under him. The right leg moved in a different direction to the left; with that, his body folded in the middle and he landed head first in the snow.

'For God's sake, please don't make me laugh' I thought, pulling my face deep into my scarf.

My father swore loudly and forcefully at the snow. He tried to support himself on his hands that were now resting on the cold ice. His face was contorted and his eyebrows covered with snow. I bit hard on my lips trying not to laugh and I told myself, not to make a wrong move, otherwise I would regret it.

Then the real father stood up. "Damned snow! Why have I had to come out with you? Can't you go and do your lousy skiing by yourself instead of dragging me out in this shit weather?"

I stood there as if a horse had kicked me. My urge to laugh had disappeared. Did I hear correctly? Who asked whom to go out and play? Typically, it seemed it was always my fault.

The skis lay in front of him and to emphasise the end of our joint outing he kicked the planks forcefully with pent up anger. However, I still got my revenge, because his scream and limping movements revealed the pain he had just inflicted on himself. I tried hard not to laugh.

"Do your own shit," he muttered and with this he hobbled back home through the snow. I was stunned, but was I surprised? No.

However, I did not want him to spoil my Christmas. After he went, I thought, I would show him how it's done. I found a small mound with a flat top, on which I balanced my skis. Gently I scrambled to the top (at the full height of one metre) and fastened my feet with the two pieces of leather straps on to the skis. Securely tight, I now stood united with my Christmas present and ready to go. I took the two ski sticks and tried to push myself downhill. There was no forward movement; only the ski tips pointed downwards and instead of descending, they lodged themselves into the soil at the foot of the snowy mound. My body was bending forward and I supported myself with the two sticks, whilst the end part of the skis pointed skywards. Helplessly, I was strapped into a hanging position, half in the air, unable to get my feet out of the clamps.

"Mutti!" I screamed. Nothing, not one curtain twitched when you needed it. After a painful and very embarrassing five minutes, I freed myself but my knees, feet and every bone in my freezing body hurt.

Later, I discovered that father had not even bought me this Christmas present, but had won it in a card game, in a pub probably together with the recorder.

'What a thoughtful father I had!'

Oh, one more thing I remember about his temper. One day he offered to play chess with me. However, I won the first and only game. He became so furious that he took the chessboard, whacked it over my head, and then accused me of cheating.

Just another example of my caring father.

CHAPTER 7

The rhythm of life

When we consider that we are all crazy, life is explained

Mark Twain

My body developed a yearly ritual. As soon as summer announced its presence, my tonsils began to swell and I was confined to bed with a high fever. My friends used me as a reliable barometer. "Heh, what's the weather forecast? What are your tonsils saying? Is it holiday time?" they smirked.

I received the traditional family medical treatment, which grandma swore up on. Apparently, it had been in use for centuries, she confirmed. As I had a very high fever, a hot water bottle and a thick covering duvet were applied to me preventing any cooling air reaching my burning body. On top of these medical procedures, I had a woollen scarf wrapped around my head to keep my neck warm. I was wearing braces in my mouth to stop my teeth growing in all directions and I looked as if I had just come from the dentist.

"That's the best treatment," grandma announced. "The boy needs to sweat it all out." I had the feeling that she did not want to prolong my young life.

During this time, families like ours received charity from an organisation called 'Mutter Hilfwerk' (help for mothers). This charity provided holidays on farms for vulnerable kids. I was selected twice for this opportunity. However, every time just before the departure I became ill and had to kiss good-bye to the holiday.

On one occasion, I made it to the departure platform at the train station but just before boarding the train, I suddenly became dizzy with high fever. I sank into the arms of my mother, and never stopped crying until we got home. All my friends looked forward to their holidays of a lifetime and disappeared in a cloud of steam, escaping from the departing train. I was so devastated that I wanted to die. I cried for two days and was not able to eat anything.

Amazingly, I did survive and as soon as I was well, again, I was told to go to the shop and get some fresh bread. Most food we purchased from a small grocery store that I started to know quite well. I enjoyed this task, as the shopkeepers were two elderly women who gave me some sweets or biscuits from time to time. Maybe they liked me or maybe they took pity on that skinny boy.

Unfortunately, on my way home, the fresh, delicate aroma of the warm bread made me forget that I to hurry up, as mother was waiting to make breakfast. Oh, the crust, the smell, the temptation, "Just take a little bit!" pleaded an enticing voice inside me. A short fight broke out within me. The temptation won. I broke off a small piece. The smell of this warm delicacy and the taste was just too much. I just could not help myself; "only one more little piece" whispered the devil's inner voice again. I gave in.

When I entered our flat, I realised that half the bread was gone. A resounding slap in the face let me know that my action was not acceptable. A red imprint of a hand on my cheek was the confirmation. Anyhow, it was a small price to pay for this delight.

Father still worked for the Hamburg Gas Board. He was in charge of reading gas meters. Our family now had a regular income. As soon as our local grocery store was sure their customers would be able to pay, they were eligible for credit. We tried to repay our loan at the end of every month when wages came in. However, I think a rather large part of father's wages found its way into some pubs.

Potatoes and coal obtained through haggling and bartering were stored in the scary cellars which all of us children feared. They had black pipes running on the ceiling that sometimes made gurgling noises, and dim lamps, which clicked off automatically, frightening us to death.

When I heard the dreaded words: "Rudi go in the cellar and get me a bucket of potatoes" I had to be quick, as I only had two minutes before the lights went off and I was left in darkness. I shivered, because many times I had run into a wall as the lights went out and I could not find the switch. On some of my visits, I felt my heart sinking into my pants. The fear of ghosts and the stories some of my friends made up about their experiences of escape from kidnapping and murder, took hold of me whilst I made the first brave steps into the unknown. I am sure I heard some voices….

The blocks of flats now were fully occupied. My friends, who were a mixture of idols and idiots, contributed to the formation of my character, which I carried with me into *'growing up'*. I knew which boys qualified as my friends. They had to be strong and protect me, as I was still considered a weakling. The only pastime for many residents was, to sit at their windows for hours. These council house spies noticed everything and nothing escaped their peering eyes. They provided the all-important gossip for curious neighbours and every bit of childish naughtiness was reported back to our parents.

*

One day I looked through the security of our newly fitted net curtains which mother had installed to save us from prying eyes.

"What is happening? What is going on?" I opened the window wide.

A large crowd had gathered in front of the allotments, which were surrounded by machines and trucks. Then more diggers, demolition equipment and a human work force completed the picture. It looked like this consortium had come to complete what the war had not been able to destroy. The machines towered threateningly in front of the small tin, wood and concrete huts like a brigade of Panzers waiting for the signal to attack.

"God damned demolition squad!" cried Herr Rabler. The sweat was running down his face, which had changed from paleness to a flaming red colour. He shook his fists and rushed from one driver to the next to see into the eyes of his enemies. His hands were scratching his grey hair in a mixture of resignation and defeat which mirrored his face and his twitching lips.

"God damned bastards! Leave us alone! What do you want from us? Who the hell has commanded and authorised this action?"

Suddenly, there was a hellish tumult. Screaming, pushing and threatening fists formed a resistance as it started to dawn on the group of old men and women that the unavoidable defeat was becoming a reality. This was the last stand of the 'ALLOTMENT ARMY'

"These bastards are as bad as the Nazis." were his last words. The reality of their superiority took hold and once more, he swung his chicken axe, but now without conviction.

His colleagues were screaming, shouting and threatening, but all to no avail as the occupiers stood their ground doing nothing, just staring. A feeling of powerlessness and helplessness overcame these ex-soldiers and prisoners of war who had returned to a destroyed homeland.

"What the hell did we fight for, losing our arms, legs and our belief in mankind?"

"WHAT FOR! WHAT FOR?" became the chant.

"Is this the price we gave our lives for?" These words were hanging in the air like a bad smell, which would not go away. In silent resignation, the pensioners took to their wheelchairs, started to walk away and mount their rusty bikes. The dream of these desperate people for a piece of land to cultivate was disappearing slowly but unavoidably. I saw tears of frustration running down these pitiful faces. These once hopeful survivors of a human catastrophe now had to reflect on another defeat.

For the last time, Herr Rabler sat on his blood stained chopping block. He looked like one of his countless victims. His shoulders were shaking. His future here been washed away, like his tears in this Hamburg rain. God did not hear his pleading or just ignored him.

Herr Rabler got up. He let his axe fall to the floor and wiped his hands on his trousers. His head sank on his chest. He was a broken man. He walked to his shed, and took his coat and now without any anger, just resigned himself to his fate.

"SHIT," he mumbled.

His subdued, depressed figure vanished and suddenly he became only a memory. He did not see me or maybe he did not want to see me.

His shadow was one of a lost generation whose suffering and sacrifice left an irrevocable impression in my heart. I was saddened, as this special friendship between our different generations disappeared like a cloud, carried away by the wind of time. I never saw him again.

GONE – LOST – FOREVER

CHAPTER 8

My education is waiting for me

I have never let my schooling interfere with my education

Mark Twain

Just before my seventh birthday in the year 1953, I confronted the inevitable: School!

The serious part of my life began and suddenly with little warning, my normal routine ended; playing and freedom now curtailed. The trick the grownups bribed me with, was a very colourful large cardboard cone filled with sweets to ease my entrapment. As a sweets loving child, I did not have the slightest chance to resist these temptations. Finally, after inspecting and eating some of the sweets I half-heartedly agreed to participate in this new adventure. Mother put a satchel on my back, filled with coloured pencils and other educational paraphernalia. To round it off, they took a photo as evidence that I willingly agreed to this journey. I clasped my cone as mother took me by the hand and steered me towards the entrance of the school.

This cathedral of learning had withstood all war time attempts to destroy it. The dark, brownish monstrosity did not radiate any kind of friendliness or welcome, and the steep, high steps felt like they were leading me up into a prison. On the top step stood a man draped in a grey suit. He tried to smile despite the chaos created by the new arrivals. No messing about here, his posture suggested 'I am the boss.' I would meet this man on numerous future occasions.

The boss gestured to my mother: "Halt, here, not one step more. It's my turn to take over".

His appearance gave the impression of a generation, which not long ago had had to deal with terrifying situations on a battlefield and had now switched to working with small children. That transition could have not been easy and it showed.

I thought my mother would defend and fight for a sympathetic outcome for her only son, but without a gesture of resistance, she accepted his command. The only thing I heard her saying was, "Bye my lovely boy, be good and well behaved"

I held frantically on to her hand.

"No, I don't want to go in there, please, please stay with me."

She pushed me gently into my future. Betrayal was the only thing that crossed my mind. She stroked my freshly brushed hair, waved good-bye and left me to my fate.

"Well, well it is not that bad, is it? I won't bite you."

My new boss tried to reassure me. With blurred eyes, I made a last attempt to reach freedom but he took my hand and led me through the enormous door. To rub salt into my wound he took my coloured school cone with all its treasures and gave it to my mother. Bribery had done its trick.

"You'll see you will like it." Mother's last words sounding from afar disappeared into my suspicious mind. Suddenly, I was in a long yellow corridor.

"You, yes you!" The gentle tone had now changed, as his finger pointed at me, "This way."

I was led into a room where a further thirty or so children were already present. Freshly washed and dressed fellow comrades, were now sitting awaiting their fate. Between the runny noses and blurry eyes, you could hear the words,

"I want my mummy."

However, the door to the outside world was shut firmly. I sat on a bench, attached to a wooden desk with a sloped surface. Even the boy sitting next to me, who occupied most of the bench and was nearly double my height and width, also had blurry eyes.

We were kept within the State School 'Langenford Grundschule' in Hamburg Barmbek, surrounded by a fence that gave the appearance of a huge enclosure. This enclosure was later to be filled with screaming and playing children, during our class breaks.

There were a number of teachers employed here with psychological damage. It was the result of fighting and killing during the war. Many of them had witnessed the death of friends and comrades and experienced the horror of complete destruction. They were still grappling with these memories. How could they suddenly change and know how to deal with small children, who needed gentle guidance into adulthood?

The classroom door opened and our heads turned around. Our chattering stopped abruptly. The hour of truth had come to reveal who would come to direct our life for some time. However, our class was in luck.

"Oh, what a lovely flock of children we have here. Good morning to all of you," announced the voice to start our academic life.

"Good morning," we replied. We knew how to behave and respond to authority as we had been given clear instructions from our parents.

A small, roundish figure with motherly features stood in front of a large desk. "I am your teacher and my name is Miss Schmidt," announced our new guardian.

I thought she looked friendly and trustworthy and her reassuring smile covered her face. Maybe this smile represented her hope of a new future. Maybe our fresh, young faces triggered in her a moment in time to be filled with laughter and the hope that our generation would be a beacon of light, and put behind the horrors of the past. After this very encouraging introduction, our learning settled in to a pleasant routine.

Every morning I got out of bed and had breakfast, which was porridge or a piece of bread with homemade jam. I then took my prepared parcel of dripping or buttered sandwiches for lunch. After a short walk, I entered into the huge, not so dark anymore, school building.

As soon as I was inside the classroom, the friendly face of Miss Schmidt brightened my day. I am sure it was not an easy task to teach our diverse assortment of children how to read and write or even add up. It needed all her professional strength, skill and patience to help us to overcome these first academic hurdles of our lives.

Only God knows where she found the patience to try to explain to me that one plus one is not three. The bigger the numbers became, the more power of persuasion was necessary to push me to understand. Gradually her patience declined many times, she had to repeat the process and her expression darkened to indicate the end of this task. However, she never hit any of us.

One day, after managing to count more numbers than I had fingers, she asked. "Who can tell me how many of us are in class today?"

"Yes, Karl?"

He started counting "One, two and three" but then the enormity of the task got the better of him and he stopped. After most of the class had had a go, someone amongst us arrived at the number thirty-two.

"Well done!" she said.

My hand shot in the air and with my fingers clicking, I tried to attract her attention.

"Yes, Rudi," she asked. "Miss, with you, we are thirty-three," I announced with a voice full of confidence and pride.

"That's right. Well done"

After this mathematical contribution, I think I became one of her favourite students.

*

All went quite well for the next two years but then grandma made a   decision that redirected my education and upbringing. Her decision was based on a lurking disaster, which had to be avoided at all costs. It was her duty in the name of God to act on His behalf. My salvation was at great risk, because our Catholic God was not present in these halls of learning, which teemed with heathens and Protestants. She therefore decided that I had to leave this place, in order to save my soul. Mother and grandma agreed that I had to enter a Catholic School, which united all believers in the only religion that in their opinion would secure my entrance into heaven. Action must be taken, in order to escape the fires of hell.

"My boy, after the summer holidays you will be attending a Catholic School," mother informed me with an authority that gave no room for objection. I must now leave this place of my well-established routine over the last two years, and go to join the chosen ones. I was to be taken out of my circle of friends and thrust into uncertainty and the unknown.

To understand the way they thought and acted to save me from damnation soon became apparent. A priest had informed my mother that she was not 'really' married in the eyes of God, as my father was a Protestant and therefore without fail, she was damned into eternal hell. I am sure it must have been an almighty shock for her to realise, if she did not act to save me, she would be responsible for condemning me into the flames of hell for all eternity.

On the last day of school, before the summer holidays, I said good-bye to my classmates. Miss Schmidt came to me and we shook hands. "Goodbye, Rudi, I wish you all the best and hope you will be happy in your new school." For a fleeting moment, I saw a hint of tenderness and sorrow in her face. I thought she might miss me.

CHAPTER 9

An ordinary young life that was often eventful

In three words I can sum up everything I have learned about life: it goes on

Robert Frost

Mother chose the Catholic St.Franziskus School, in order to save and educate me. I started there in my third year of schooling decorated with the very Christian surname of Heiland *(translates as Saviour, Redeemer also mentioned as Son of God).*

Well, if this does not reek of disaster, then I do not know what does. A boy named Heiland in a Catholic School did not augur too well. I already had the feeling that the balance was tipping against me and I was certainly tested, in the first few days. My teacher introduced me by name to my new classmates and as soon as the word 'Heiland' left his lips, the room filled with sniggering voices.

At break time, an inquisitive bunch of pupils surrounded me. I sized them up and concluded that it was not worthwhile even considering any form of defence, as most of them were taller and stronger.

"Hey you, what's your name?" I knew what was in their mind and what their aim was. I kept silent, shrugged my shoulders, and tried to escape.

A blow into my ribs let me know that ignoring them would not work.

"Well?" Pause. "Do we have to wait?"

"Heiland," the smallest kid shouted, followed by hysterical laughter. "Heiland, like the son of God?" hissed one of the group.

"Well, answer!" Another blow released a stream of tears from me.

"Answer, are you Heiland, the son of God?"

A blow to my head released the answer they wanted to hear.

My resistance broke, I nodded "Yes," I whispered.

"Good, as you are Jesus we want to see a miracle," screamed the laughing gang. "Here are some sweets. Now make as many as you can out of these, so all of us can have some. Schnell, schnell."

A boy started pressing some sweets into my hand. His dark rimmed glasses had slipped off his nose with all the excitement he thought he had created. Now without his glasses, I realised that one of his eyes looked to the left and the other to the right. This picture of his vulnerability eased my pain for a split second. His wet hands now pressed my hand and forced an imprint of the sweets into my flesh.

"No!" I cried uncontrollably. I shook my head. "It won't work, I cannot do it," I yelled.

"Liar, do it!" shouted some gang members and then they started to slap my face. A final kick made me slide to the floor and suddenly I was alone. After a while I recovered and realised the sweets were still in my hand, and with a smile I put them into my pocket. I went to the toilet and tried to dry the wet patch on my trousers that had occurred during my torture.

WELCOME TO THE CATHOLIC SCHOOL.

"What the hell was going on down there?" our teacher asked, "and you, Rudi why are you crying?"

"Oh, I just slipped and fell, but all the other boys wanted to help me because I'm new here."

With just this one sentence, I had made a whole gang of new friends.

At the end of this school day I skipped home, singing along with my ex tormentors.

Most of us, by whatever means or strategies we use, climbed the ladder of education. Some students who did not do very well during a school year had to repeat that same year. Many of these psychologically damaged, because of their chaotic home life. There were children missing their fathers, who never came back from the war. Some mothers had chosen the wrong replacement husband, even ones who did not accept their children. Many of them ended up in a 'Special School', which we kids called, 'Doofen Schule.' (*School for idiots*) We were just not ready to be considerate or polite but preferred calling names and insults at each other. It also seemed that the motto of some teachers was, 'they are stupid and there is nothing more we can do' and lost interest in teaching and helping them.

Many of these teachers, who were returning from the war, had their own problems, which might have prevented them nurturing this unfortunate group of students into the next phase of their education. Maybe it was the beginning of a selection process, to determine our place in society and our future.

Our Catholic priest performed our religious education, with very limited teaching skills. He was also the big chief next door at the adjacent church. He was the ears and eyes of God to whom I had to confess my sins. I am sure he recognised each sinner and remember the sins we had, to disclose to him during confession.

Now was his chance to test the sincerity of my MEA CULPA, MEA MAXIMA CULPA, (My guilt), and decide the level of punishment he would dish out. I had to learn phrases from the catechism to recite in front of him. My pulsating, painful, knuckles and red coloured palms were evidence that he did not agree with my performance. Everybody feared his threatening ruler or stick. It must have been his way to tell us that through beating we must not forget to become good Catholics.

Many times, I had the pleasure of enjoying additional education in detention. Ten pages of repeated writing down, "I must learn to behave myself," or, "I am not allowed to talk without putting my hand up and being invited to speak" was nothing I could not manage. After an hour or two, the exercise book was inspected, ticked off, and I was released.

"Where have you been?" my mother would ask. There was no real concern in her voice on such a day. "Oh, I just played football with some friends" was my short answer.

The eleven plus exam lay in wait and lurked like an enemy with all its hostility in front of me. This was the moment where my life and education could be launched into a new orbit, and an opportunity to keep my nose in front and maybe to become as clever and successful as my fellow classmates were. I was informed that learning and knowledge were the coloured pencils of life with which to create the picture of my future success.

However, based on my previous exam records, my chances of success were not great. Most of my annual school certificates had the same sentence: 'Rudi is working to the best of his ability' while many of my classmates got the phrase 'could do better. '

The time came and I sat down to complete the exam paper.

"You cannot do this," my brain kept telling me. Perspiration, a dry mouth and total exhaustion took hold of me. Breathlessness was overwhelming me like a roaring wave, drowning all my rational and logical thinking. This Goddamn piece of paper that was staring at me and waiting for my answer was getting wet from the beads of sweat, dripping from my forehead. Time was ticking relentlessly on. The clock hands were racing within my closed eyes. The throbbing and thumping in my head was becoming ever louder, settling in my ears. I had no means of stopping this inner noise. I felt sick and nausea overcame me.

I felt paralysed. I wanted to scream.

My brain came to a grinding halt, and any pathetic attempt at reactivation came to nothing. Finally, the bell rang and signalled the end of the torture of a failed exam. However, I heaved a sigh of relief.

"Well, how did it go?" asked my mother after I came home from school.

"Oh, I don't know, I think it was okay" I lied.

"Well, we will see" and with this mother continued the washing up.

The summer break came and went again without any sign of a holiday with my family.

Then one day after coming back home from school, mother called "Rudi, there is a letter for you, I think it is the eleven plus result. I want you to open it." Mother patted my head expectantly.

After a little while grandma asked, "Well, don't you want to open it?" I avoided answering her question.

A brown envelope, leaning against a used cup of coffee, was staring at me. The clean crocheted tablecloth paved the way to the reckoning, but I already knew the answer, which would determine my future.

Disgruntled, I tore the envelope open.

I pretended that I was reading the content but one word immediately hit my eyes, 'LEIDER…' (Sorry)

It was what I expected but still, this moment of reality was painful and humiliating. Not surprisingly the pain I felt was real and started to hurt me, even if it was foreseeable. I began to cry.

"What is the matter my boy?" Mother took the confirmed notice of rejection and failure from my hands. She read it long and thoughtfully. Then there was a pause. She sat down, folding her trembling hands into her apron. Those beautiful hands that gave me so much comfort and love. I saw it in her face, it was not hurt or sorrow, only disappointment that clouded her tender face and lingered in her sad eyes.

How I did yearn at that moment to be the boy she would have liked to see? I was not able to give her the light of hope she so deserved. After all the darkness she had been through, I trembled and cried inside.

She sighed. "Well, there is nothing we can do now. It was not to be." She sighed again, but this time a bit deeper and louder. "What should we do?" she shook her head and repeated the phrase as if to confirm her helplessness.

Then came her answer. No, it was a quote, which will haunt me for the rest of my life.

"It doesn't matter anyway as the grammar school is really only for rich children. It is for the children of civil servants and managers. Yes it is for them, not for us, only for the others."

Now sorrow and real disappointment covered her face, because in her mind I had missed the chance to enter into this higher stratum of society. She had tried to find an excuse and explain to herself that nothing out of the ordinary had taken place, and that everything had taken its normal course.

Mother wiped her nose and dried her eyes, got up and said, "Get some potatoes out of the cellar," and with this comment, my position in her mind, in her world was sealed. I was trapped, and belonged to a working class family that lived in a block of council flats and would know my place in society. There has always been an established rank and order.

It was like this in the past and still is now, and in her eyes, I had missed stepping out of it.

I survived the final years of my education without permanent damage. This was mainly due to my skills of copying, adjusting and passing off my neighbour's works as my own.

After the exam and the disappointing result, this working class boy was now fully able to enjoy the summer.

The school days passed and did not interfere with my young carefree life, after I quickly digested the failure of the eleven-plus exam. I was taught to believe that God would predetermine our life's directions. However, sometimes you reach a point in life where you have the chance to change that path and decide your own destiny, but it is not always to your advantage.

At this time of my school life, the most important person trying to guide me was Herr Blaschke. He wore the title headmaster with pride, and he was the one who had the say during my remaining school years. Although for him, I was only a statistic, like everybody else, he was approachable and trustworthy.

One day we enjoyed a beautiful summer's day and the sun shone on Hamburg, which was not the norm. This weather confused me and presented complications, which I had to face. The problem was that we had choir practice that day. The sun enticed me with its warmth through the open class windows. In my mind, I faced a dilemma. Do I take part in the choir practice or go to the outdoor swimming pool? What a question and what a decision! As happens so often in a young life, the answer came before the rational decision.

The class walked in line into the sports hall and most choir members were deep in conversation. Just a short distance before the hall doors my friend Günter and I came to a pre-planned agreement. We moved through the left corridor without changing our steps or tempo, and walked out of the school towards the sun, swimming pool and freedom. After a short while, we were convinced that our absence had gone unnoticed.

"Well, that was easy," laughed Günter.

"Ha, ha nobody realised anything. It would have been shit to sing on such a beautiful day, no way!" I said. We skipped over the rubble and ruins of former houses, threw stones at ruined walls, and ran towards our destination. We were so proud and satisfied that we had managed to escape the choir practice. In mutual admiration, we slapped each other's shoulders.

Afterwards, on reflection we were both of the opinion that the sunshine was to blame for what we had to endure. We were sure that we were not to blame.

What we did not hear, immersed in our own delight and euphoria, was the squeaking sound of a fast approaching bicycle. The wildly pedalling legs of our headmaster, Herr Blaschke were pushing disaster towards us. Suddenly, a shadow appeared above us. Unfortunately, we noticed this too late to escape his outstretched hand. An open fist clutched my collar, leaving me gasping for breath. In this moment of overwhelming shock, I did not notice that the fist had now left my collar and had changed into a flat weapon, which connected with my face. 'SMACK': the sound rang in my ears, at the same time as the pain hit my cheeks. Then, with lightning speed, the hand was back on my collar. The whole procedure happened so fast that I did not have the time to wipe the tears from my face. Herr Blaschke then repeated the same procedure on Günter.

"What the hell do you think you are doing? Who do you think you are? What is written on the school timetable, heh?" He screamed.

Staring at us, his face bristling with anger, he waited for an answer. "Swimming or choir, eh? What is it?"

We mumbled some words, which did not satisfy him. "I can't hear you. Speak up!" His threatening hand reinforced his anger.

"Choir," was my attempted answer.

"I can't hear anything," he hissed close to our faces.

I felt a small shower of spittle as he was gasping for breath, which made me realise that he was furious.

"Choir," I tried to say it louder.

"Choir! What?" He screamed at me.

"Choir, Herr Blaschke," I answered trying to save myself from further punishment.

"Good and now go back to the sports hall. I will cycle back and if I don't see you there within five minutes, well only God can help you!"

His dark, piercing eyes confirmed his threat and with that, he shook his head, swung his legs over the saddle, and disappeared between the ruins. We ran as quickly as our legs could carry us. I became aware that even with a runny nose, I was able to cover a considerable distance in a short time, and arrived in less than the five minutes requested.

As soon as we arrived in our dishevelled state, Günter and I stood in front facing the school choir. Then a masterpiece of psychological punishment, meant as a warning to all pupils. With a loud and clear voice, our tormentor declared,

"Dear fellow pupils, we have the pleasure of listening to two gentlemen, Rudi and, Günter, who will now perform a French composition called 'Le coq est mort', translated it is known as the cock is dead."

What a bastard! I formed a fist.

The faces of the whole choir were visibly smirking, and this developed into laughter. This cynical display caused a seething feeling inside me that I was helpless to repress. Their howling laughter sounded like a tornado coming from afar. Günter and I stood with lowered heads, feeling insulted and hurt in front of everyone.

On my way home, after this agonising experience, I tried frantically to forget this humiliation and to pretend that all was fine on this beautiful sunny day. Experience had taught me that if it became apparent that I was in trouble at school, the already painful punishment from the headmaster would result in a second helping from my father. Quite honestly, one hiding was enough. As I entered the front door, I immediately knew something was wrong. Somehow, our household had already heard about this incident. God knows how the school bush telegraph had transmitted this news.

Mother greeted me with "What the hell were you thinking of, skipping class? Just wait until your father comes home."

I realised that the in-house jury had already come to a verdict. I went to a part of the flat where I thought I could hide.

"Where are you? Come here!" I heard the thundering voice of my father. "What in the devil's name did you think you were doing? Absconding from school?" His red face displayed an uncontrollable, raging anger. "I will show you how to obey your teachers you God damned rascal. What have you got to say?"

"I am so sorry. It will never happen again," I blurted, because I was aware of the punishment I would receive. It had happened before when he had been in such a state of raging anger, and any plea for forgiveness was now too late. At this point, his control was beyond any human sanity.

He took the carpet beater, which stood in a corner. I felt his hand grabbing my collar and with one push, I landed on a chair, my shorts ripped off me, exposing my soon to be wet underpants. The carpet beater lashed my backside and even my hands, which I used to try to protect myself were beaten red. Eventually, my painful screams alarmed my mother because she knew what he was capable of when he was in such a mood. She appeared, shocked and worried.

"Hans, Hans, leave the boy alone, enough, enough," she screamed at him, begging him to stop.

Maybe she remembered that this drama had happened before. On one previous occasion mother had had to stop him beating me, as blood was seeping through my swollen backside and afterwards, it was near impossible for me to walk.

My soaking wet face, drenched with tears and with an overwhelming feeling of complete submission, was a picture of total rejection and collapse. My hands slid over my buttocks trying somehow to ease the pain. That burning fire in my backside would prevent me from sitting down for some time to come.

Later, lying in bed with the pillow absorbing my tears, I promised myself, if ever I have my own children, and I'm ever tempted to dish out such abuse, so God be my witness, lock me in the deepest dungeon and throw away the key.'

*

School days often weighed heavy against my casual daily life, and sometimes interrupted it with detention and homework.

Often, my behaviour left my teachers no choice but to act decisively. Sometimes the class stretched teacher's patience to breaking point, in the daily struggle to decide the winner and loser between teacher and pupil.

One of those occasions occurred when a classmate told our teacher, Herr Meisner, that he had witnessed a fight between two pupils, which all of our class had encouraged and supported, even though we had no idea what the fight was all about. Hearing this, Herr Meisner declared that our behaviour was wrong and not acceptable. As a result, we would all have a detention at the end of school.

Our strongman and appointed leader Bernd, protested, "That is not fair. That goes too far and has nothing to do with us. We were not involved in this scrum. We will not accept this lying down. We will show him that we are no push over and will not sit here for an additional hour!"

After a short consultation, he nominated Paul and Karl to go to the greengrocer's and buy a bag of garlic. We all nodded in unison and Bernd collected some donations.

"So, when we get the garlic, we are all eating a full lump of it. That stinks nicely and Herr Meisner has to sit with us for an hour," he announced.

We could hardly stand upright with laughter and Paul and Karl left during the next lunchbreak to purchase our smelly weapon. Well, that was the theory anyhow.

The hour of reckoning arrived and we munched the garlic. The stench floated through the classroom. All eyes fixed on the door, where Herr Meisner would appear. We saw the handle move and with one push the door opened and the fearsome Herr Meisner entered the classroom. He was not easy to recognise as our eyes were streaming from the smell of garlic. He just stood there in front of us and laughed loudly.

"Well, well, my dear class let me put it this way, if any of you are thinking of opening one window they will have to deal with me personally. Furthermore, I will send a letter to your parents describing your behaviour. Is that understood?" He asked in a relaxed voice. "Well, I do not hear anything. Is that understood?" he asked, his voice becoming louder, but somehow sounding still relaxed.

"Yes Herr Meisner," we mumbled.

"Oh, by the way, as garlic is apparently good for your health, I have decided it will be to your benefit to enjoy an additional hour in this healthy environment. I will see you all in two hours from now. How you explain the delay to your parents is up to you. Oh, and one last thing, you have to write the following sentence at least fifty times, in your best handwriting: "I love garlic, because it is healthy and therefore very good for me, "and with this, he closed the door and was gone. I had the feeling we were being   taught a lesson. Anyhow, life at school carried on. Our behaviour did not change.

Mother was used to me being late from time to time and on this occasion she only asked, " What is that smell?" shaking her head.

We smoked cigarettes in the toilets and were caught and punished by teachers. This circle of events continued for some time. I don't think we were the nicest bunch of students and this surely contributed to the near nervous breakdowns of some of our teachers. One of our teachers became so depressed and disillusioned that the headmaster had no choice but to move him to another school.

CHAPTER 10

My first steps into the world of commerce

*The superior man understands what is right; the inferior man
understands what will sell*

Confucius

As happens many times in life, tragedy can also create some
positive opportunities. The hated demolition brigade that was
intending to clear the allotments stopped due to some internal
government directive. The rumour was that they going to use
the land to build a large school after the clearance of the
allotments. This was a signal for us to explore the partly
demolished sheds and small brick houses, to look for
countless treasures. "Scrap metal," was our battle cry. Within
the rubble and ruins lay iron, steel and copper which my
friends and I could sell. There were many travelling rag and
bone men pushing their carts around, looking for anything
that could be bought for cash. The new Germany had issued
the Deutsche Mark, a hard currency to replace the million to
one inflationary Reich Mark, decorated with Hitler's head.

We identified iron girders, wooden planks and copper wires, all moneymaking materials that we exchanged for sweets and bags of broken biscuits. A full paper bag of broken biscuits cost 10 Pfennig *(less than half a penny)*. Some of us decided to buy cigarettes and cigars rather than sweets, as we thought this would make us look more grownup. We all agreed because the forbidden was exciting. Anyhow, I had the insurance and security that all my sins, would be forgiven in confession. That was the great advantage of belonging to the Catholic club.

Conspiracy and secrecy, reinforced with an oath between us, had forged our group much closer. This closeness could only be broken if our parents found out what we were up to.

Now, our chosen group leader, started to inspect the sheds and small buildings to decide where to start. We picked out iron girders, iron bars, copper pipes and cables. These valuable goods were loaded on bikes, carts and wheelbarrows and transported to a trusted scrap metal dealer. Holding our breath, we followed the pointer of the scale until it stopped to indicate the extent of our wealth. Our appointed accountant gratefully received the agreed amount. Cash is king and we felt like kings! We stood very close to our accountant, as trust was not yet fully developed. One never knew if temptation would get hold of him and he might run off with our cash.

We overcame the illegal purchases of cigars with statements such as "No, no, they are not for me; they are for my father, of course." I am certain the shopkeeper smelled a rat, but I am sure he did not have many sleepless nights about this transaction.

Off we went on our bikes to a lake next to Hamburg's large cemetery where we could hide in the reeds. We shared the cash, and our first successful job was celebrated with a big cigar. After this thing was set alight, everybody took a puff. Only a weakling did not inhale fully. Now it was my turn. I took the already wet tip into my mouth to draw on it like a big boy, as I had just observed the others doing. Suddenly, big clouds darkened my vision. Red and blue circles covered my eyes and exploded in my head. I started to be sick. The inhaled vapour brought a stream of tears to my eyes. The sight of my spitting cough ignited a screaming laughter from my comrades. Sour, acidic mucus spattered uncontrollably from my mouth, all over my shirt. A whirlwind took hold of me and I sank puking on the floor. Only continued laughter from my 'so called' friends assured me that I was still alive. I tried to sit up again after my dizziness diminished slightly. Unfortunately, the others did not help me as they were still rolling about on the floor laughing.

After a while, my vision cleared and clinging onto my bike, I started to get up. I then realised a feeling, which had not been there before. With every little step, a foul smell confirmed what I feared. "Oh shit," I mumbled, confirming the stinking reality. I carefully walked further into the reeds and threw my underpants into the lake. Only one thought dashed through my brain. "How on earth will I explain the loss of my pants to my parents?"

I arrived home and the unmistakable smell gave away my secret straight away. Even my unconvincing explanation did not save me from a good hiding. I quickly realised smoking is bad for your health.

*

One day we sat between the ready to be demolished ruins and selected our targets. We looked at walls and ceilings and inspected corner pillars, which had once protected the meagre belongings of their owners. We chose a small concrete shed where half the walls were missing, and detected an exposed iron girder that supported the brickwork over a door. The promise of more cash made our hearts beat faster. The only problem I realised was that the girder was half covered with bricks, which we had to remove. I went for a closer inspection. While I was standing below the door, my demolition partner threw a chunk of concrete to loosen all the bricks, which then collapsed in a cloud of falling rubble onto my head. Through the cloud of dust, the result became visible. I slowly realised what had just happened. A deep open wound formed on top of my head and the blood shot straight out, blood flowing over my eyes and face, and was only halted by my flat hand covering the wound. My face formed a grimace, with drying blood and a coating of dust all over it. My flickering wet eyes completed the picture of horror. I was in such shock that I could not even sit down. I looked for my partner but he had disappeared. I staggered through the dust that was still falling from the spot where the wall had been. I felt terrible, and I began the journey home, to find some form of help or comfort. Then I realised that my upper body was nearly naked, blood stained and extremely dirty as my shirt was completely torn. With my right hand, I tried to stop the fountain of blood but a trickle found its way through my ripped shirt collar.

I got home and rang the bell. It seemed like an eternity until I heard my mother's familiar footsteps. She opened the door and stood deep-rooted, frozen, as if made out of stone. Her hand clasped the door handle. A distorted face was staring at me. Not a word left her lips.

"Mum I have…" I began my explanation and with this, I took my hand from the top of my head to confirm what had happened to me. A gush of blood shot over my hair and face.

My mother started to sway and let out a choking scream. Her hand slid off the door handle and with a crash, she collapsed unconscious onto the floor. When she came round after a few seconds, we both started to cry.

A neighbour, who had just walked by, helped her get up, took her into the flat and laid her on the sofa. He then offered her a glass of schnapps, which was always a well-used medication. Now, my mother recovered and was able to look after me. After a good wash, a full facial bandage was wound around my head.

"Shall we get him to a hospital?" I heard somebody suggesting. "You must be joking, what for?" was the answer.

Later, after I had described what had taken place, my mother punished me with two weeks confinement to our flat. I was lucky that she did not inform my father; otherwise, the carpet beater would have connected with my bottom again. That was the end of my demolition career.

*

However, when one door closes another one opens. My more serious commercial career started at an early age.

The British army was now running the show in our part of occupied Germany, known as 'The British Sector'. Now they were acting as administrators and apart from still catching Nazis, they were trying to help us get by. Suddenly, there were a number of British military trucks appearing around our streets. A translator told us that every family would receive so called 'Care Parcels'. These packets contained cheese, margarine and butter. For the first time in my life, I saw orange coloured cheese. Very quickly, I became aware that butter was the most valuable commodity in the Care Parcel. With this in mind, I swopped some cheese and margarine for butter. With luck and some begging gestures, I got extra portions of butter, which I then sold for profit.

I did not feel any shame that I profited from these Care Parcels. I learned very quickly that money made the world go round and I wanted to be a passenger on this roundabout.

CHAPTER 11

A look through the window of the past

Ultimately, the oldest desire is fleeing to escape death

J.R.R. Tolkien

Unfortunately, even with all the good and positive events that happened to our New Nation, it was not easy or impossible for many to escape the dark shadows of history. It felt as if the past was tapping the person in question on the shoulder with its memories of misery and sorrow.

"You remember me? Do you still know who I am? I am your past!"

Fear invaded the souls of these poor creatures, threw its anchor into their flesh and opened deep embedded wounds. Surprised and shocked these victims held their breath. Their brains started working and developed a consciousness of the unforgettable horror. It would suddenly appear like a mirage they prayed to forget but could not. For many there was only one way out of this nightmare, a self-inflicted death. These victims were not able to close the invisible door of their deeply imbedded burden.

I witnessed the '*looking through the window of the past*' spectacle at first hand. It screwed my mind up even more as I was unable to digest this trauma. Father, mother and grandma with me in tow, all dressed in Sunday's finest outfits, boarded tram number 6 to take us to a large assembly hall.

Walkways led us through pleasant, parklike gardens with a magnificent display of beautiful, colourful flowers, greeting the assembling participants.

Across the steel door, gleaming with its freshly polished glass, hung a large poster:

OSTPREUSSEN – HEIMAT TREFFEN

(EAST PRUSSIA –HOMELAND MEETING)

We elbowed our way through a crowd of displaced (ex-) refugees from East Prussia now in search of news, answers and maybe closure.

"Hang on, wait a minute; I'm just looking for Kurt, he reserved our table". Kurt was my father's brother. After a short while, we saw him waving to us through the crowd. I was greeted by some of these lost souls with a pat on my head or with a comment, "Oh what a nice boy!"

They ordered beer and schnapps for the men and wine for the attending women. I stood amidst a cloud of cigarette smoke, an aroma of consumed alcohol and was overcome by the noise and hugging all around me.

Now the seriousness of the event started to materialise:

After the first introductions and greetings of lost friends and relatives, the reality of the event took an unstoppable centre stage. It was time for those present to recall the known and even worse to reveal the still unknown, the most horrendous experiences that these human beings had suffered. Long suppressed memories suddenly washed over the vast crowd like a raging tsunami. Individual friends and relatives started to open a book that each had left locked away for some time, and with tears in their eyes, they began to opened chapters of their wretched lives. These now endlessly recounted stories would never leave me ever, even though I was not one of these suffering people. I will carry these testimonies with me into my hopefully better future.

Those present settled at their reserved tables. After a welcome speech from the chairman and the introduction of the planned schedule, he invited a speaker on to the podium to recall their last days at their home in East Prussia.

The first contribution came from an elegant, well-dressed woman. She started with her voice full of pain. It looked as if she needed to gather all her strength to be heard.

"We were scared of any reprisals from the Russian army in revenge for the terrifying warfare the German troops had inflicted on the Soviet Nation." She paused and looked around to register the impact of her words. She continued, "Rumours circulated about what the Soviet troops were capable of. The first wave of the troops consisted of peasants, mainly from Mongolia. These were wild soldiers, fighting for six years on the frontline, looting the 'liberated' cities, raping women and killing whomever they chose. Hundreds of thousands of families had fled from East Prussia and it became one of the larges exoduses in modern times. Some jumped on the few still running trains; others were still waiting because the Nazi authorities had forbidden any retreat." She paused again.

At that point, I remembered my mother saying that our family had also been unable to flee because of this cruel order announced by the remaining loyal Nazi administration.

She continued, "Families with their small children had to leave all their belongings with only a few minute's notice. These poor people had to leave their farms and homes."

Mother and oma looked at each other and memories of this horrendous moment filled their eyes with tears.

"They fled in long queues with heavily laden carts, some with packed sledges but most on foot. East Prussia covered with a thick blanket of snow and the thermometer indicated at least twenty degrees below zero. Many of our friends and families did not make it and many little babies died in their mother's arms." Her tears demanded another pause for the audience to digest these spoken words.

Still, the woman tried to continue. "The Soviets reached the coast very quickly and the overland escape route was cut off. The only way out was the road north in the direction of the Baltic Sea to the entrance of The HAFF."

NOTE: THE HAFF is a part of the Baltic Sea and it is 80 kilometres long and up to 18 kilometres wide. A 70 kilometre long and two kilometre wide stretch of land separates THE HAFF from the Baltic Sea.

"Many of the refugees tried to flee towards the West over the small strip of land between the HAFF and the Baltic Sea which started to be under attack from the Russian troops. Thousands of refugees were hungry and freezing. Some families took refuge anywhere on their way in sport halls, churches and even private houses but many had to sleep outside in atrocious conditions. People were fighting in queues in front of the few open bakeries for just a morsel of bread. At the cemetery we saw the dead being laid out in the open ground around the mortuary," she concluded, as exhaustion took his toll.

While these bitter words fell into the silence of those present, the images of the praying hands and weeping eyes left an overpowering imprint upon me. The whispering of, "May God have mercy upon us" hung over like a cloud. The faces of my parents, relatives and friends, reliving these moments, darkened still further this atmosphere of death and commonly experienced horror.

"Dear God!" Another voice from a graceful, petite woman who was invited to give her version of events. Her troubled voice floated through the room. "Dear God, I don't know if I can bring myself to recall this trauma," she took a deep breath and stood up.

Her voice was laden with pain, but nonetheless, she started to open the dark account of her exodus: "Get out, get out, run, flee; shouts and screams of complete panic filled our home. We just made it, or we would have been swept away by those triumphant and pillaging hordes," she sighed. "Mother and I were the first to run out of the house. We could not find my sister, we anticipated that she had run outside already, and we left but could not see her. We had no choice, either going back into the house and be raped and killed or join the ever-growing stream of fleeing neighbours."

Tears streamed down this gentle face marked by the scars of history. "Thank God, we were united eventually but my sister told me, she was still in our house, hiding, when she heard the front door being broken down. From her hide-away she witnessed our grandmother and our little sister being raped." Her speech halted by heavy swallowing and sobbing. "Afterwards they gripped my sister by her legs and threw her against the walls of our once beloved home where she was granted the liberation of death. We never saw our grandmother again," she concluded with breaking voice.

One could only imagine what had taken place during this recalled ordeal by witnessing the pain and sorrow in this contorted figure.

"This apparently occurred shortly after these soldiers had destroyed a nunnery and raped and then killed anyone they could get hold of." She sat down, not moving, only weeping quietly to herself.

On our table sat an old man. He was dressed in a jacket and tie. His face had a stern expression and he reminded me of a man that had grown up connected with the countryside. His strong hands gave the impression of a once resolute person. Maybe he was a farmer but his face was now a window, through which one could see his despair and misery. His voice had a strong, but gentle tone.

"I think we must have been some of the last to cross the Haff," he started. "It must have been minus twenty degrees. As there were thousands on the march, many had to find a path over the frozen water of the Haff. The ice did carry our belongings and us. Our suitcases became heavier and heavier by the hour. We were close to freezing to death but we all had only one thought in mind, just go forward and in God's name do not fall into the hands of these terrifying troops." His slightly opened mouth twitched as if it hesitated to release the formed words. "Behind us we saw farmers trying to save what they had worked for all their lives. Their wagons, piled high, were pulled by suffering horses. The frozen waters that carried our lives were filled with hundreds or even thousands on the march to safety."

He paused.

"Suddenly we heard a sound which I will never forget in my life. It was a piercing, singing sound." His words disappeared in a cry that rattled the breathless, stillness in the hall and confirmed the insanity of this macabre situation. He wiped his eyes and continued: "A sudden cracking and breaking noise spread through us and then…Oh my God….the ice swallowed everything behind us. Whole families disappeared screaming beneath the ice, mothers, fathers and their warmly wrapped children. We witnessed two little girls and their brother, all gone!" He stopped.

"Their mother was kneeling on the edge of the ice, trying helplessly to reach her disappearing children. Other mothers were still holding their dead babies, silently sobbing. There was no time to grieve, no time to say good-bye. A picture of sheer depression and defeat shook us to the core. Mothers and some old people sat down in the snow and ice, unable to take any more of this hopelessness, and died. Their frozen corpses, like monuments mirrored the unimaginable horror. Thousands of these tragedies will stay deeply embedded in the hearts of the nation, for many years to come." He took a deep breath, and continued. "In this chaos of death, we saw approaching Russian fighter planes, machine gunning and killing hundreds of helpless refugees and horses. Hundreds of dead bodies were lying amongst the slaughtered horses. A devastating picture of total carnage took place in front of our eyes. Only wordless, silent prayers escaped now from the survivors frozen lips, floating towards the grey and icy sky. However, the trek moved on regardless."

He shook his head, as his words, framed a picture of this terrible memory.

"It was as if Satan himself was trying to tell us that what our nation had permitted to be done in the last few years had come home to punish us." He looked with haunted, empty eyes at his audience. "When there is so much death everywhere around you, life and death becomes an inseparable grey mist. The screams of our nightmares are heard throughout the land and the survivors of this all-consuming war, who committed suicide, will remain unknown. During the escape over the Haff, fifty thousand people including thousands of children, mothers and old folks lost their lives," he concluded.

I swallowed hard as it was unusual and very moving for me to see a grown man cry. My mother and grandma were sobbing, as were many other listeners, reliving their personal nightmares.

The hours of crying from relived memories of these horrendous times finally ended. The beer and schnapps eased the pain a little bit. After making promises to friends, and newly rediscovered relatives and neighbours to keep in touch, we started our journey home. Maybe this exchange of remembrance and suffering had been an important way of cleansing and of trying to make a clean break from the past.

*

The war was now over. The grey cloud of this human failure vanished slowly. Believe me, humanity will learn from its mistakes,

Fingers crossed.

Since the beginning of time, a veil of forgiveness and forgetfulness has settled over the dark history of humanity, together with ignorance and rose-tinted coloured glasses and a big fat lie 'it will never happen again.'

I sincerely wished our family would now be able to put a well-deserved closure upon this nightmare but would never forget these horrendous events. Let us pray the human race will take this historical trauma as a lesson to guide the new generations to a better future.

We all now live in hope and time will tell if humankind has learned from its mistakes of the past.

Now it was my future, full of hope and expectation. From now on all things will be better.

Not until we are lost do we begin to find ourselves.

– Henry David Thoreau

CHAPTER 12

However, life goes on

If life were predictable it would cease to be life, and be without flavor

Eleanor Roosevelt

In general, my childhood was reasonably happy. I played in the road and in the courtyards of the gigantic block of flats, we called home, without any worries or watching out for cars. Some summers were often nice and warm, perfect for visiting the open swimming pool 'Am Dulsberg'. The Hamburg winter delighted me with snow and ice when we used to race our sledges on the frozen canals. One of my greatest thrills was to climb trees as high as possible and swing on the thinnest branches. How I did not break any limbs, I do not know. I gave my mother several near heart attacks.

We could not understand why the grown-ups were always shaking their heads and moaning: "Yes, yes, when we were young things were different. The weather was much nicer and the kids of today are just very spoilt and ungrateful." It seems time is a healer and allowed this head shaking generation to forget what they had just gone through. Now they tried to push the last twenty years into the background of history. I was sure the experience of the grim and nasty past was slowly sliding into a macabre fairy-tale, but I know, we will hear the same moaning in the future: "When we were young…!"

The social housing community organised paper lantern parades. Weather and darkness permitting, our little group of over excited children would march around the block of flats when the gas streetlights started shining. We saved our pocket money to buy these paper lanterns decorated with the sun and the moon or stars. The shimmer of flaming candles inside the paper balloons created a wonderful mysterious atmosphere. The happy procession of yodelling and shouting kids would carry the decorated, glowing lanterns, hanging on wooden sticks, around our neighbourhood. During such evenings, between seven and eight o'clock, our world was perfect. When we were on the move, we sang wholeheartedly a specific song: "Lantern, lantern, the sun, the moon and the stars."

However, sometimes the whole platoon would come to a complete standstill because one of the paper balloons had caught fire. The bearer of the blazing ball would burst into tears and still holding his smouldering stick, he would disappear into his mother's arms.

Every two years the adults also organized a 'Block fest' *(Courtyard festival)* within the safety of our council community. The inner courtyard decorated with colourful lights and lanterns and a wooden dancefloor installed. Loudspeakers blared out music and sometimes we even listened to a live band, which got the old and young dancing together. Long wooden benches invited neighbours to eat, drink, dance to the music and sing loudly. It created a camaraderie, which took away all thoughts of the past and the unknown future for some hours. Homemade schnapps and cases of beer inevitably affected the swaying crowd. Encouraged by the consumed alcohol, some neighbours danced a bit closer together than they should have and held each other tighter than their watching partners would have liked. In some cases, a man's hand made contact with a dancing breast. This was the signal for some uproar and an enforced musical break, which often ended with a black eye and a bloody nose for the guilty party. However, with a little bit of time and more alcohol the two fighting cocks would calm down and were soon reunited, embracing each other, whilst emptying another bottle together. A jointly bellowed song would announce the end of this fight and their slurred words would proclaim their eternal friendship. 'Love your neighbour!

What fun we had witnessing these grown-ups!'   Anyhow, everything was forgotten by the next day. Well, not by everybody.

"In God's name why did you behave like that yesterday how embarrassing?"   My mother told father the next day.

"Unbelievable, how could you do that and of all things with the wife of Walter?"   Grandma added her bit.

"What Me? I did that   I can't remember anything like that," my father groaned, fighting a massive headache. His head was still swimming in a pool of schnapps and beer, and the pain was pounding in his brain.

Traces of Alka-Seltzer on his hardly moving lips were evidence of his inner fight. "Oh God, I feel so bad and don't scream so loud." He released a deep breath and moaned, "I promise you I will never drink again! I have had enough. No one can stand this!" His aim was to convince his audience that he was only a victim of the event and not the culprit. "It was Heinz who started with this shit schnapps. I did not want to drink it, but, no, he insisted!" It is true Heinz broke the neck of the first bottle, but now father had conveniently forgotten that most of the subsequent liquid had come from his stash.

"That's me done, finished with this crap. I'm not drinking again!"

Well, mother and grandma had heard all this before, and knew what he was like and so walked away. He only honoured his statement until that evening.

In this summer of change, a most remarkable event, gripped Germany and remembered for years to come.

In 1942 and 1946, there were no football World Cup tournaments, because The Third Reich had started a different game, called World War Number Two. In 1950, Germany had not been invited to participate, as the rest of the world was not sure, if we had now become a nice and peace loving nation. Then in 1954, as the wounds of the war started to heal, the German national team was invited and qualified to take part in the World Cup tournament in Switzerland.

My father's friend was one of the few people in our council block that possessed a TV. He invited us to watch the final in his very cramped, cigarette smoke- filled room, which slowly filled with empty beer bottles. Germany won the World Cup, against all the odds, and this occasion became known as *The Miracle of Bern.'* Grown men started to hug and kiss each other and were crying like little children. It felt as if a pressure valve had opened, releasing the stress and emotion, after what this generation had suffered. I witnessed the first signs of re-emerging national pride. Between all the jubilation of cries and tears, a new confidence and hope was spreading through the country. A nation still on its knees was making its first steps towards national identity, a new future and being part of the International Community, instigated by a football game.

*

Later that year, on Sunday the Second Advent, father came up with a wonderful surprise. "We all are going to the Hamburg Christmas Market, the whole family."

Wow! My sister and I stared at him. We both were thinking the same. 'What's the catch?'

Father's friend Heinz had a VW Transporter equipped with two rows of benches. Heinz's wife, my mother and sister were sitting on the backbench and I sat squashed between Heinz, the driver, and my father, as we drove off.

So far so good, the only thing nobody noticed was that Heinz was completely drunk. We drove towards the market in a very festive mood and suddenly there was a loud scream.

"Watch out! Oh no!!!!" We had crashed head on into an oncoming car. The only thing I can remember was that the three women flew off their benches and crashed onto our front bench. There were no seat belts in those days and they ended up lying on the floor with blood running from their knees and hands.

As the VW transporter had no bonnet, the impact was catastrophic. After the enormous crash and noise, I opened my eyes and realised that I was the only one left still sitting on the bench. No mark, no injury, not even a scratch, nothing.

(The second intervention of my guardian angel.)

My father had disappeared flying through the front window, complete with the windscreen. Our drunken driver Heinz had unwillingly exited through the driver's door. Both men had landed on the road and sustained life threatening head and body injuries. The passengers in the other car also suffered frightening injuries, as did their little dachshund, which was thrown against the windscreen. They were taken to hospital by ambulance. Later I was brought home into the arms of my grandmother. At least we made the news in Hamburg's newspapers.

Father and his (now) ex-friend Heinz were confined to a hospital for some months. Later we learned that Heinz was transferred to a different institution. He served some weeks there to consider why it is not advisable to drink and drive.

MERRY CHRISTMAS – OR NOT?

CHAPTER 13

Fashion presents the image of the day

Fashion is a form of ugliness so intolerable that we have to alter it

Oscar Wilde

The architects of our social home base must have had children themselves, because within the large courtyard they had installed some luxuries for us kids. There were swings, large sand pit and last, but not least, a swimming pool, constructed of dark brown tiles. There were three steps, which enticed us to climb down to swim or play as soon as the weather permitted.

On weekends as early as seven o'clock, there would be a group of us waiting to get into the water. The pool was in the middle of hundreds of flats and yet we did not consider enjoying our activities quietly. We invented games, but during the explanation of the rules, nobody would listen. Some had their heads already under water, so we communicated in forms of screams, shouts and wild gesticulations. We realised very quickly that some residents had different ideas of early morning relaxation. Windows opened in various places and a torrent of abuse flew through the air. Heads, which two minutes before had been firmly absorbed in sleepy dreams, appeared at windows,

"Are you crazy to make such a racket? Can you all shut your God damn mouths, otherwise I am coming down to give you a good hiding," shouted a friend of my father.

"Bloody riff-raff, making such a noise, so early in the morning, shut your traps, otherwise…!"

The threats kept hanging in the air, as the onlookers started conversations between themselves.

"I can't believe it's seven in the morning and this rabble screams like crazy. Every day I go to work and when you have a day off and can lie in, these idiots wake you up," shouted a well-known disabled veteran. "Let me come down and sort you out, you'll regret it!" he howled.

We just laughed, because we knew he was a drunkard and was no threat to us. Both his legs were missing and he only could use a wheelchair. However, sometimes when he was not completely drunk he was quite pleasant to us.

On Sunday mornings, mother and grandma dressed up and got me ready to go to church. As a good Catholic family, it was compulsory to visit this Christian clubhouse every Sunday. Somehow, mother had rescued an item of clothing she thought would look divine on my tender body. This piece of ugliness was made of brown velvet. To top it all it was a girl's outfit. The jacket, crowned with a white laced frilly collar, had crocheted sleeves. The matching shorts that finished just above my knees completed this very inappropriate outfit.

My friends teased me with comments such as "You look as if you are from a planet where only girls live". My image as a demolisher of ruins had totally disappeared with this hideous outfit. However, my family and relatives saw a different picture and serenaded me with hymns of sheer delight.

"Oh, doesn't the boy look beautiful! How sweet!" Or even "What a charming child! If only his grandfather could see him!"

Waves of Germany's most popular 4711 perfume wafted through the house, as mother and oma finished the final touches for their rendezvous with God.

"Mother, I'll just go and wait outside," I announced.

"No," she demanded. "You stay here otherwise you might…" I only heard part of some of her mumbling, as I was already gone. I walked over to the pool and I put my hand in to feel if the water was cold, but my foot slipped on one of the wet steps. I tried frantically to grab something to gain my balance. God himself or one of his angels must have given me the final push, for unfortunately, there was nothing to hold onto.

SPLASH! Head first, with my freshly combed hair I landed in the water. My head broke through the moving waves to grasp some air.

My Catholic uniform completely immersed in the floods of the swimming pool. I spat out the swallowed water and desperately coughing, tried to climb out of the pool.

With hindsight, perhaps it would have been a better idea to stay submerged. As soon as I was back on dry land, I began to tremble furiously, and not only because of the cold water. I looked like a drowned rat. The water dripped off my velvet suit, which was beginning to shrink and press on my wet skin. My hair was hanging in strands down my face. I only had one shoe on as the other was floating gently on the water. I stood in the middle of an expanding puddle and did not hear her approaching. A hand grabbed me and with one acrobatic move, I landed face down on grandma's knees and her hands worked hard on my wet bottom.

Many heads appeared in the windows above to enjoy this spectacle from a front row seat. I had provided a different wakeup call that was worthwhile getting up for. This audience encouraged grandma and every smack accompanied with resounding applause and laughter.

"Jesus, Maria that serves him right!" shouted somebody from the second floor window. "Now, finally he is getting a good thumping, God damn rascal. This is payback time for him for disturbing us in the early mornings!"

HALLELUJAH! Somebody cried.

The show ended with a final smack to the applause of the audience. My grandma dragged me across the courtyard straight into the bathroom and helped me, not very gently, out of my velvet 'swimsuit.'

However, as so often happens, a drama has its sunny side and this painful performance ended in a lucky triumph for me. I looked at the ruined pieces of clothing, which now were lying on the floor and thought,' this horrible ugliness is torn, unwearable, it is gone, kaput.' My internal jubilation was overwhelming.

FREE! I felt liberated.

Even my family benefitted from my dramatic action, as grandma was able to use some of the fragments to make some cleaning rags. I witnessed the early stages of the concept of recycling!

*

'Unusual fashion, from unusual people' rewarded me with some weird and wonderful moments. On certain days, an organ grinder came to entertain us to make some money. He was dressed in a top hat and tails (which surely had seen better times), revealing a white shirt and a golden waistcoat. A red scarf with white spots decorated his neck. A smallish monkey dressed in a red frock sat on his hand organ, secured by a small chain. He tried to bite the taunting children or pinch their sweets if they came too near. The squeaking wheels and the sound of music announced the duo's arrival, even before they came into view. At a guess, the music man must have been fifty years old or maybe he was in his thirties. His marked face did not reveal his real age but told a story of a turbulent past.

During his musical performance, he took his top hat and tried to collect donations. The little monkey tried his best to entice us to part with some of our pocket money by performing swirls and jumps. As soon as the man took his hat off, it was the sign for us children to look on the floor, avoiding any eye contact and plan our exit route.

After playing more music, the organ grinder conceded that his attempt to make money around our block of flats was not financially viable. After few more attempts with the same result, he gave up and disappeared.

However, men offering to sharpen knives, as well as women selling wooden clothes pegs soon replaced him. Some of the men had long dark coats touching their boots, whilst many of the women wore long, colourful dresses, and often crowned with matching headscarves.

"Be careful with that lot, they are gypsies" grandma warned me. It was an open-ended piece of advice, as it was never explained why we should not trust these people. Every time they came to our flats, I ran home to ask mother if she had some knives that needed sharpening or to tell her the price of pegs. Other kids also collected knives to be sharpened. The more we would collect the more we could watch the sparks flying from the grindstone.

Every day as darkness slowly descended, I would wait for the dreaded man on his bike, whose job it was to switch on the street gaslights. His appearance announced the end of my playing day. It was unavoidable that within minutes our window would open and mother's voice commanded,

"Come on now boy, it's time to come in, understand?"

I stamped my feet, clenched a fist and grumbled. 'Shit! It's always me to be the first to have to go inside!'

"Mother, can I just…." I tried to beg, but was immediately cut short. "No, you are coming in, now!"

"We only want to finish our game, it won't be long," I pleaded.

"I said you are coming in, now!" she shouted back.

Still complaining and grumpy, I said good-bye to my playmates and with my head hanging low, I disappeared into our family HQ.

CHAPTER 14

Happiness is a blue bike

Whoever is happy will make others happy too

Anne Frank

My birthday was approaching. I was counting the time before the big day. Finally, the special birthday song I heard every year woke me up, coming from a record player, placed next to my pull out bed.

I was rubbing my eyes and squinting against the flame of the candles, embedded in a chocolate cake. Mother began with the usual ritual of congratulations. "Happy birthday my son," followed by my sister and grandma. My father had already gone to work. His latest job promotion involved reading gas meters in and around the red light district of St. Pauli.

"Mutti, where are my presents?" My prying eyes searched the room.

"Oh," said mother with masked embarrassment, "Is there nothing?"

"No," I replied disappointed, "Only the cake."

"Oh my God, oma did we forget Rudi's birthday?"

Now I began to really panic. How would I explain to my friends that I had no presents to open?

"Ah, I think there is something in the hallway," grandma's voice echoed from behind the door.

RELIEF – SALVATION

I jumped out of bed, ran into the hallway and stopped as if somebody had suddenly put the brakes on. I stood still for a minute, completely flabbergasted and unable to close my mouth. There, in front of me, leaning against the wall, stood a brand-new bike, sparkling in its sky-blue colours.

"That is for me?" I cried. My hands pressed against my cheeks, unable to contain my happiness and surprise. Nodding female heads confirmed that I was now the proud owner of the most beautiful bike in the whole wide world.

Quickly I got dressed and, of course, forgot to wash and brush my teeth. Nobody could shout at me, not on my birthday! Off I ran into the street to practise riding this most beautiful, blue bike, decorated with a silver stripe. I pushed my present very carefully down the street, holding on to the chrome handlebar, decorated with a bell. The bike was nearly as tall as I was. "It has to last for some years" was mother's explanation, with a smile.

Over time, after my first wobbling attempts, I improved and finally I was able to match the advanced skills of my friends and join their outings. The next practice was the 'hands free' exercise that often ended in near misses, which only were avoided after quickly clenching the handlebar.

One day I was cycling with my friends from a side street into a main road and did not notice that the tramline was sharing the road with me. My bobble hat was firmly on my head and my hands were off the handlebars. My bike was gliding over the shining, wet cobblestones. Suddenly, the front wheel caught in the tramline. I took off, flying from my saddle straight towards a lamppost. At the same moment as my body made contact with the lamppost, all the lights went out in my head. Instinctively I tried to hold on to the post but I slowly slid towards the earth and landed in a dog's deposit. After pushing the bike back home, all my friends helped me to repair the damage so that my parents would not notice.

My bike and I were inseparable partners and every possible free minute I went riding with my friends. After long and careful checks that I was safe, my mother allowed me to cycle the forty minutes to school, through Hamburg's traffic. It also became a useful tool in earning extra pocket money. Each Saturday morning I would deliver newspapers, packed on my bike, to households in our area.

HAPPINESS was a small word to express my feelings.

CHAPTER 15

Jesus calls me for duty

Religion is what people tell you to believe

R H H Heiland

I was thirteen years old, and it was obvious that, to be a good Catholic, I had to earn my heavenly entrance ticket and become an altar boy. It was grandma's belief, that through my Christian duty as a servant of God, He would consider me for my salvation. Of course, we were made to believe, that this opportunity would only be granted to Catholics. All other followers of different forms of belief would have a problem in squeezing through the pearly gates of heaven.

Well, let us see who is right. I am not sure; we will find out.

Every Sunday without fail, I stood finely groomed in my finest clothes waiting for the trip to our spiritual rescue centre. Mother and grandma, with their freshly ironed outfits and matching hats, were my ever present companions. I was watched like a hawk, since my previous mishap, when I fell into the swimming pool.

Of course, father had an excuse, as his birth certificate showed he was persona non grata as a Protestant and therefore not allowed to attend this holy gathering of Catholics. He was a member of the competition. The boss in Rome, who decreed, that a marriage between a Catholic and a Protestant was void in the eyes of the Catholic Church, confirmed this doctrine. Amen.

It seems that these shepherds of all religions and beliefs considered their members to be like flocks of sheep, safely herded into their own pens. In order to prevent them from jumping over the imaginary fence, to find out if the grass is greener on the other side.

Most of the time we walked to a chapel in the Catholic Hospital called Marienkrankenhaus in Hamburg Eilbek where I fulfilled my duty as an altar boy. It was a pleasant little place of worship, with a proper organ. It was never a problem to get into, as we were well known altar boys.

One afternoon my fellow altar boy and I sneaked into the chapel. We started up the organ and played some well-known jazz tunes, beginning with, 'When the saints go marching in'. An alarmed duty nun appeared and showed us the way out with some harsh words.

*

One Christmas Eve we celebrated a Midnight Mass. Every mass was conducted in Latin, which we had to learn. On this occasion we were four boys all dressed in red frocks and white flowing shirts directing the ceremony of salvation. We rang the bells; we swung the frankincense containers secured on chains and we served wine and water when required by Father Best. I stood by him when he distributed the Body of Christ at the Holy Communion. With his trembling hands, he put the blessed wafer between the lips of the receiver and I held a golden plate below, just in case he dropped any crumbs of Jesus.

Amongst the core congregation were patients with broken limbs and other handicaps, praying for a speedy recovery. There were, however, some disadvantages to being an altar boy, placed in the limelight at this festivity. We were always the first to receive the Holy Communion. It was a deadly sin to accept the Body of Christ while you were in trouble with God. In this instance, Father Best offered me the 'Body of Christ' and I bowed my head in a gesture of refusal and with this I proclaimed for the whole congregation to see, I have sinned!

As it would have been unusual at my young age to murder somebody or rob a bank, there was only one conclusion in some sharp-minded observers, as to what God had witnessed. I am sure many were thinking that I did not keep my hands above the duvet. I looked into the congregation and mumbled:

"He, that is without sin among you, let him cast the first stone."

For a moment, it made me feel better.

It might have dawned on some of those present praying and singing that the obstacles of sexual impurity had been thrown into my adolescent path. The sexual obstacle course of life had started for me. Full of embarrassment and remorse, I tried to regain my composure and engaged in the Latin based ritual.

However, the duty to serve God also had its funny side and the pendulum swung from embarrassment to an outright comedy, for us anyway.

The first part of the Midnight Mass passed by uneventfully. We were praying and singing and all the Hallelujahs were flying towards heaven. Then it was time for Father Best to spread his joyful Christmas message. It was a mixture of encouraging words of praise and love, sometimes interrupted with a show of a warning finger. You cannot have a sermon without the warning finger.

We retreated into the sacristy.

While we were sitting and talking, one bright spark suggested we should also celebrate Christmas with a bottle of Hungarian Mass wine, which was standing on a nearby shelf.

The cork left the bottle, and the bottle made the rounds until its contents disappeared. As this bottle was not blessed, to drink it would not be counted as a sin, and therefore we would not be excommunicated.

Slowly but surely, the white walls of the sacristy did not seem so pale. The joyful message of Christmas took hold of us. The bottle was empty just as we heard the final words of Father Best's sermon, "and now my dear friends, God bestowed us with a new beginning, in the name of the Father, the Son and the Holy Spirit. Amen"

When we heard the Amen, panic spread through the room, as to where we could hide the empty bottle. I quickly put it between the full ones. That resulted later in a complaint to the supplier. We four drunken servants of God tried to form an orderly line to return to the main stage. Father Best, the most good-natured man known to humankind, greeted us with a smile. He took our responsive smirking smiles as a confirmation that his sermon had delivered a joyful message that had inspired us on our way to salvation.

I was responsible for filling the frankincense container. With my little shovel, I loaded an extra-large quantity of frankincense grains into the vessel. I am sure one of the Three Kings would have been proud of me. It was now the duty of my assistant to spread this holy aroma into the congregation, which he accomplished with wild swings of the container. Within a short while, we heard the Christmas audience coughing through the large clouds of frankincense. The congregation wrestled with handkerchiefs and gasped for air. The only one not affected was Father Best who was absorbed in his prayers. Suddenly, there was a dull sound behind us. One of the women had collapsed in the pew. Only the reaction of her singing neighbour prevented serious damage. Within minutes, she was fully conscious and sang as if nothing had happened.

What finally amused and entertained us, was a large, bluebottle fly that whizzed around, as if the holy aromas had also affected its flight path. When this big fly landed on my forehead, I could not hit it without nearly losing my balance, due to the effects of the alcohol. Suddenly a knock in my ribs reactivated my concentration. "Heh, can you see that?" my friend whispered.

"No. Where? What?" I asked. He nodded in the direction of the large golden Bible positioned in the middle of the altar. "Look, on the book."

A mischievous grin covered my face, as the bluebottle transfixed all four of us. We looked at each other and the fight to suppress the laughing began. Breathless, we watched the unfolding process. Father Best's voice proclaimed "In nomine domini patris et filii et spiritus sancti," and with his final word, he was in the process of closing the Bible. His eyes pointed in Heaven's direction and therefore he did not see or anticipated anything, as he closed the Golden Book. The bluebottle, which was trying to escape its inevitable fate, was caught in mid-flight, and finally found its resting place between the holy pages.

That was the last straw for us. Heady from the alcohol we nearly collapsed with smirking laughter. It was all too much to contain. We acted in unison. Not a bended knee or the sign of the cross was attempted and an escape from the altar decided. The door to the sacristy offered a rescuing exit. Our faces were wet with tears of laughter. We tried to calm down but every time we opened the door, to go back to serve the last part of our duty we had to stop as hysterical laughter took hold of us again. Finally, the madness was conquered and we made our way back to the altar. With blurry eyes, we joined in with the whole congregation, singing in full voice: 'Silent Night, Holy Night all is calm....'

Back in the sacristy, Father Best blessed us, and said, "I know it is overwhelming to witness such a wonderful and emotional celebration. We are all blessed to experience such a beautiful night." With this, he released us.

My mother was waiting for me. "What in God's name was going on today?" she enquired.

"Oh, Thomas got some incense clouds in his eyes which hurt him so much that we had to go into the sacristy to help him," I lied.

"Well, well" she replied. Somehow I had the feeling she did not believe me.

"Why are you speaking so slowly?" She looked at me suspiciously. "Listen, next time you have to be more careful with the incense. We were all coughing and one person fell unconscious and collapsed."

I went to bed still laughing under the duvet and thought; this was a joyful Christmas in the true sense of its word.

Wow, did I sleep well that night!

'Where there is faith there is also laughter'

Martin Luther

CHAPTER 16

Moving up in the world

Looking back can be encouraging, if you believe you can look forward

R H H Heiland

The years of childhood, with all their beauty as well as their negatives are the most important years for later life. In our naivety and limited capacity, we often try to influence their direction, but with little effect. Life's path often determined by conditional circumstances, like where and when you were born. Social factors, and most importantly, our family are usually the greatest influences during our upbringing.

As for my family, we moved from Hamburg - Barmbek to the district of Eilbek, a more affluent middle class part of the city. My father left his job at the Gas Board and the family took over a 'Kolonialwaren' shop *(grocery store)*. It was father's idea to create a self-sufficient future, as he was a qualified master baker and had previous experience in this own business in his father's bakery shop in Allenstein.

I made new friends who encouraged me to join a table tennis club and later also a handball team. I helped in the shop, mainly delivering goods that the women could not or did not want to carry. This provided me with some pocket money.

Then came the summer, when I experienced an overwhelming feeling of helplessness and disappointment that inexplicably took hold of me. Loneliness was suffocating me and this memory lives in my head and will stay with me forever. I now lived in a world of civil servants, managers and small business owners. The school holidays had begun and my street started to empty. "Where are you going on holidays this year?" my friends would ask. I did not answer, just shook my head.

As my friends disappeared with their cars packed with suitcases, I sat alone on a small wall in front of our shop. Tears streaming from my eyes. I clenched my fists and looked into an unreachable distance. What I experienced in my younger years became an everlasting painful memory. My parents never owned a car and therefore I had never been on a family holiday.

*

Later on, joining the Boy Scouts enriched my early teenage years. We learned how to tie knots, went on excursions and camping weekends, and taught to respect nature and our fellow compatriots. I forged some strong friendships during that time.

On one occasion during our Whitsun holidays, we cycled sixty kilometres to the Ratzeburg Lake, where we built a campsite and shared the cooking and washing up. We were swimming in the lake, even though the temperature at the beginning of June was not warm in North Germany. We were told, what does not break you makes you stronger. (Sound familiar?)

I was still one of the smallest boys, pretending to be strong and without fear, and often volunteered for tasks that required guts and determination, to fend off any attempt of being bullied.

Even though we were a large, restless group of youngsters, there was only ever one accident of any note to report. We invented a game called 'Test of Courage,' which involved having to detect and apprehend one person lurking somewhere in the woods in complete darkness at the lakeside. One member of the group became spooked by the darkness and surroundings and, with a piercing scream, started running back to the camp. Unfortunately, for him, he did not notice a well-established oak tree and ran head first into it. Suddenly, torchlights started to flicker everywhere to assess the damage. Our comrade was lying in the damp grass with a bloody head. In the true spirit of the Boy Scout motto 'Be prepared!' We quickly brought a self-made stretcher and carried him back to the camp. The next day he was fully functioning again although decorated with a white head bandage, visible in the dark, thank goodness.

In late summer, I enjoyed another camp in the deep Bavarian forest. On this occasion, the endurance bar was set much higher. The task was a two-day solo trip. Equipped with a map I had to identify and visit some marked locations, and then find a place to spend one night.

I was alone, and I got completely lost on the very first day. I was not able to read the map, and therefore it was useless to me. I found myself walking on a small path through some dense forest without any direction at all. Suddenly I saw a toll-bar, with a painted red and white sign:

STOP – You are entering the Republic of Czechoslovakia.

I got very scared as the daily news informed us, that we were at the height of the Cold War. I turned on my heels and ran as fast as my legs could carry me away from this barrier. I finally arrived at a farm and the owner allowed me to sleep in a shed amongst the straw bales that night. Next morning I washed in a well, and then once again was on my way and arrived somehow back at our camp.

I met a boy called Paul during one of these outings and we became friends. We realised that we only lived a few doors apart in Hamburg and decided to keep in touch.

Paul and I decided to go on our own holiday trip back to the Bavarian forest, but told our parents we were going on a Boy Scout holiday. We decided to hitch hike to South Germany and use our uniforms as a sign of displaying trust, which gave us an advantage over other fellow hitchhikers. We slept some nights in the fresh air under a blanket of stars or in sheds kindly provided by some charitable souls. We accepted an offer of a lift to Salzburg in Austria even though we knew our money was running out.

We arrived in Salzburg without a penny. We were hungry, thirsty and after some searching, we found a nunnery by chance. We queued outside in a long line alongside homeless people and alcoholics, to receive food and drinks from the charitable sisters. After this, we decided it was time to make our way back home.

Back home during our next troop meeting, we found out we had been expelled from the Boy Scouts. The scoutmaster had somehow discovered that we had worn our uniforms illegally for our own gain. Paul then told me that one of the boy scouts had asked him, if he could come with us on the trip, but Paul said no, it was a secret. This boy must have told the scout leader about us. It hardly affected me, as my life started to take another direction.

One of the highlights of my teenage years was joining a band. I was mesmerised by the rhythm drummers created. I saved every pfennig and took lessons from the senior drummer who played in the North German Radio Orchestra. I searched to join a band and I was so excited, to be accepted as a drummer. I bought some old drums and Bernd, our bandleader, helped me paint and repair them. We performed at school and church dances and even got gigs in some pubs in Hamburg. It was an exciting time, which I enjoyed immensely. Unfortunately, most of the girls had only eyes for the singer.

CHAPTER 17

The first step into the real life

Life is too important to be taken seriously

Oscar Wilde

My school years ended in April 1962 at the age of fifteen. I received my final release school certificate, which was marked with grades of near failures. I left the Catholic Institution without shedding a tear. Paul's parents and mine gave us permission to go on holiday in Scandinavia on our own. Maybe it was just them heaving a sigh of relief that we had both finished our school years without any lasting damage.

Paul's father even drove us to the ferry port in Travemuende, where we boarded the boat to Trelleborg in Sweden for our next adventure. There we were, two boys just fifteen years old, planning to hitch hike through Scandinavia. The reality of what we were undertaking started to kick in, as we got ready to sleep on the chairs on board the ferry. With all our saved pocket money, enriched by our parent's donations, and all our possessions stuffed into our rucksacks, we looked forward to the trip.

On board we started chatting to a businessman, who kindly invited us to dinner. More importantly, he offered to help us on the way to our first destination, Stockholm, by giving us a lift in his car. We thanked him and said good-bye at our first stop in Malmoe. After some days staying in youth hostels in Malmoe and Gothenburg, we arrived in Stockholm. We met some fellow travellers who gave us advice about where to go, what to see and how to save money. Paul and I went to the famous amusement park Tivoli, listened to British rock bands and enjoyed the funfair.

I had my first encounter of innocent, youthful love. Her name was Gill Karlstroem. Her blonde hair and sparkling blue eyes enchanted me. She lived with her parents in Lidingoe by the sea, just outside Stockholm. We met each other a couple of times in the city and Gill told me that her parents would like to meet me. I went by tram to her home and introduced myself. Later we sat together on the beach under a red evening sky and my first meaningful kiss took place. I fell in love as only a fifteen-year-old can and experienced a feeling of overwhelming emotion. My youthful innocence was as still precious as a diamond. She introduced me to her parents who spoke not a word of German, which matched my lack of Swedish. It was a very silent, slightly embarrassing afternoon, where our communication was by polite nods. Her mother offered me lemonade, which I took thankfully with my only

Swedish word: "Tack." Her mother smiled and tried to help and further my language skills with "Tack sa mycket."

I went back the next day, as it was our last day in Stockholm. Gill and I went to the same beach to enjoy the waves and the screams of the seagulls. We lay there silently holding hands with childlike affection, knowing we would never see each other again. Some years later, during another trip to Sweden, I found out that Gill was married and had two children.

Our next destination was Norway.

Again, we experienced a wave of good, friendly people who gave us lifts, food and shelter. However, mostly we rested in youth hostels. Norway was so incredibly expensive that our visit became a short one. As our meagre purse started to empty rapidly, we decided to retreat towards our sea crossing in Trelleborg.

The hitch hiking then became difficult. It seemed that nobody wanted to give us a lift. Finally, a sympathetic driver took pity and drove us a stretch further towards our destination. However, he dropped us off before he went his own way, at a place that was totally off the beaten track with few passing cars. After many hours without a drink or food, which felt like an eternity, we successfully flagged down a lorry. Exhausted and tired, we climbed into the driver's warm cabin. Very quickly, it became dark and there was nothing to see but forest, no houses, no lights, nothing for miles.

Paul was slumped next to the door, while I was stuck between him and the driver. The language barrier created a silence in which Paul immediately fell asleep. I was also fighting to keep my eyes open and my chin settled from time to time on my chest.

An hour and a bit into the journey I was jolted out of my sleep with the realisation that, our knight of the road was anything but a knight. His hand was trying to squeeze between my legs and he tried to get his sweaty fingers into my pants. Suddenly, I was completely awake.

"You fucking bastard! Take your damned hand off me!" I screamed. I did not give a shit if he understood German or not. I hit Paul in the ribs and screamed at him to wake up. With one hand, I fought with this bastard making the lorry swerve and with the other; I tried to open the cab door. Finally, the driver slowed down and we were able to jump out of this hellhole, whilst the lorry was still moving.

We stood in complete blackness in the middle of nowhere. Only the silhouettes of swaying trees were recognisable and the sound of the night creatures made us fearful of any sleep. In the end, we just lay down on the forest floor until dawn released us from our nightmare.

We had learnt a harsh lesson, which both of us would not forget in a hurry.

On the brighter side of life, we had experienced human compassion and kindness during this trip.

We found our way back to the ferry port in Trelleborg and got on the boat back to Travemuende, where Paul's father was collecting us.

CHAPTER 18

The beginning of the end of our family

Love knows not its own depth until the hour of separation

Kahlil Gibran

My education over, I was destined to enter into the world of business. The German nation was counting on me to participate in strengthening the economy and to take part in the ongoing 'Wirtschaftswunder' (*Economic Miracle*). I started an apprenticeship with an import company based in the centre of Hamburg.

At first, people in offices and businesses seemed to find it difficult to take me seriously, as I still looked like a schoolchild.

Hamburg had very cold winters, the lake and canals in the centre of the city were often frozen. One winter I visited the Christmas Market, with a fun fair, stalls and refreshments, set on the frozen ice of the Alster Lake. It felt a bit unusual, having a ride in a carousel, standing with hundreds of people on the ice of the lake, in the centre of Hamburg.

As I lived near a canal, sometimes, instead of using the underground train, I would ice skate to work. I soon became accustomed to the daily routine of office work and was often sent to the port in Hamburg to inspect and collect samples of honey, imported from many exotic countries. The honey was stored in small canisters.

On the night of the 16th and 17th of February 1962, Hamburg experienced devastating floods. Over three hundred people died and many houses and businesses destroyed. A large consignment of canisters filled with honey was stored in warehouses in the port and following the floods, declared as not fit for human consumption. I found a way to get four of these canisters and took them home. I then asked friends and family if they had any spare jars, and filled them with the delicious honey and sold them. This kept me in pocket money for some time.

Thank goodness, even though the honey had been declared not fit for human consumption, nobody fell ill or died. On the contrary, many people came back for more, because I was able to undercut all supermarket prices.

*

Later that year, I was on a hiking holiday with some friends and the future looked bright. Suddenly, without any warning a fundamental tragedy took place that shook my world to its core. It took hold of me, pulled me away from any rational thinking and tried to destroy my faith and beliefs. It was like a blow coming from an invisible enemy against which I had no defence. A blanket of horror, which I was unable to throw off, engulfed me. As often happens, the book of an unavoidable fate opens its first page with a trivial form of notification. "Rudi, could you please come home?" grandma asked on the telephone.

"Why now? I am having such a good time here. I am still on holiday."

"Please come as soon as you can. Your mother is ill and has been taken into hospital." I heard grandma's sad voice pleading. I thought I could visualise suppressed tears in her request. I felt sick. I tried to make sense out of this message and through the mist of my turbulent emotion, I mumbled, "Mutti." That was all I could say.

Wet sweat masked my forehead and my whole body started to shake. Suddenly, I became aware that it was very serious. In this harrowing moment, I had an intuition that something life changing had happened.

My quivering lips started to form words that I wanted to scream into the world, but only my inner feelings dealt with it. I held on to a railing to support my shaking legs.

"What's the matter? Dear God, you are as white as a sheet. Have you seen a ghost?" somebody asked. I did not answer, I simply turned around and disappeared into the depths of the darkness of my mind, slipping into my own world. I quietly packed my small case and walked out of my dream holiday. Without a word of goodbye, I made my way to the station and boarded a train. The noise of the clicking wheels counted the hours and minutes of my journey home and my blank eyes did not notice the passing countryside. I did not register anything. NOTHING!

The journey from the station to my home conducted in painful silence. Inside the flat grandma informed me with a choking voice of what to expect. Not one word of hope offered, only resignation and grief filled the room. It was like a poisonous snake that kills everything in its path and leaves nothing living behind. In the twilight of grief and sorrow, I realised that grandma would lose her daughter, her last child and I would be robbed of my rock, my guardian and the guiding light of my young life.

"Well, it is too late to visit Mutti today. We will go to see her in the morning and surprise her. I have not told her yet that you are back."

After the emptiness of our depressing evening meal, during which most of the food never left the plate, I suffered a sleepless night. Only the glimmer of the rising morning light rescued me from this trauma.

"Come" she whispered. "Let's go."

She placed her tender hands in mine and with that; she united the bond of our family. With a small squeeze of her hand, she confirmed that the understanding and protection that grandma and mother had provided me during my childhood would continue, even in the darkest hours of despair.

Silently we made our way into the unavoidable. Grandma's hand, which I gratefully accepted, gave me some strength. We entered the Catholic Marienkrankenhaus (*St. Mary Hospital*). The gesture of the ward sister immediately suggested that all hope had disappeared. I could see it in her face, without a word spoken. We walked into the ward reserved for the terminally ill, the dying. The eerie silence and the smell of disinfectant, combined with the dimmed lights, gave everything the appearance of death. Mother had been moved into a private room, her final worldly resting place.

My shaking hands covered in sweat, as I reached for the door handle and quietly opened the door, and entered the room. With trembling steps, I approached her bed. Between the white sheets lay a person I had problems in identifying as 'Meine Mutter'. (My Mother). Gone was the beautiful, tender and elegant person who had been polite, loving and proud throughout her life. A mother so graceful and wise, always there for me, ready to give advice and guide me on the right path.

This icon now reduced to a skeleton with blue and black bruises inflicted by endless morphine injections. Her arms no longer had the strength to offer comfort, protection or loving embraces. Mother was like a human shell eaten away by cancer. With pleading eyes gazing into emptiness, she pleaded, 'Let me go, free me from this pain, please release me.'

At this sight, my eyes swelled up with tears and mother became a blurred image. A little nudge from oma reminded me to restrain myself and not disclose my inner feelings. However, even grandma was fighting with her emotions to control the flow of tears, doomed to outlive her own daughter. Now after the loss of her own two sons, she was the one to witness the end of our tragic family.

"Rudi, say hello to your mother and let her know you are here." I slowly moved towards mother's bed.

"Hello Mutti" I whispered, as I bent very carefully over to be near her face.

"How are you?" This stupid phrase escaped my lips.

"Mutti," I repeated. My lips touched her face.

Nothing! No reaction.

Her morphine-transfixed eyes slowly opened looking through me unknowingly. She did not recognise her son. "Mutti!" I leaned over her, kissed her tenderly and thought I detected a fleeting flickering in her eyes. Some of my tears fell on her face. I tried to kiss them away. These carefully placed kisses and the stroking of her face were my only way to thank her for my upbringing in difficult times and for all that, she had done for me. I believed she accepted my thank you, as our faces gently touched. Now mother and son were united. For the last time on this planet, we were ONE.

"Mutti, I love you so much. Please don't leave me." I placed a final kiss on her cold lips.

"THANK YOU FOR EVERYTHING," I whispered in my last good-bye.

Even death that stood next to us was waiting a little while longer.

In this final tender farewell, only a mother and her child can feel this sacred union. It was a moment of holy belief that our souls will never separate, not here on earth, or in all eternity.

I was broken and wounded. I turned around and walked out of her life, forever. My tears were now streaming endlessly. I could not tolerate my pain anymore and collapsed sobbing in a dark corner. My head rested on my knees and, without realizing it, I had curled up into the foetal position, the same position in which I had started life in my mother's womb. Grandma shook my shoulder gently and we made our way back home, which would never be the same again.

The next morning the telephone rang at seven o'clock. The shocking and expected message confirmed the death of 'MEINE MUTTI.'

I was just sixteen years old and robbed of my mother.

*

My father now saw an opportunity to be in charge of our diminished family. It looked as if he already planned his future after mother's death. Cracks appeared even before my mother's burial. An unavoidable break-up was in sight after he let slip that he had a lady friend. What was she like to excite him so much? Was she young and beautiful? Where did she come from?

He had replaced his wife with a small, roundish woman. Maybe she could fulfil his sexual needs. Maybe she was an excellent cook or she could provide him with wealth, which had remained out of his reach all his life? Maybe she would not shout at him when he came home drunk, but would instead have comforting words as she helped him out of his beer and schnapp soaked trousers. God knows! Well, it did not matter, as our ways would soon part.

He was determined to fulfil a selfish wish to make his life easier and decided to clear grandma and me out of his way. Grandma was first. He told her clearly that her function in this family was not wanted or needed anymore.

Another tearful goodbye took place, as grandma was pushed unceremoniously out of the family and the home she had looked after, her whole life. She thankfully found rescue and peace in a care home in Hamburg, managed by nuns, where her life ended some years later.

The last familiar and trusted face disappeared out of my life. I felt alone, cheated.

My mother had died at the end of November and suddenly Christmas was upon us. Decorations and seasonal holiday spirit spread through the neighbourhood but nobody outside could have suspected the ice-cold atmosphere that lurked within our walls. No baubles or even the smallest piece of tinsel brightened our home.

My mother was dead. My grandmother kicked out. Suddenly, without any indication or warning something hit me like a bombshell. It happened the day before Christmas Eve the most important family day of the year.

"By the way, I am going to Margaret's tonight to celebrate Christmas with her," father mentioned without any emotion. "You can use the flat over Christmas, if you want. What are your plans?" He asked without any interest. Barely listening to my reply, he turned around to walk away.

This single sentence changed my life and cemented the unavoidable end of our family. His announcement hit me like a train of unimaginable force. I felt abandoned, violated and alone. I felt sick.

With raised fists, in an uncontrollable leap, I was on him and screamed. "You are not leaving me alone on Christmas Eve; you can't do that, not after all that has happened!" I tried to breathe. "I know you don't give a second thought about our family and about me." I was gasping for words, "I will kill you if you leave me! "I don't give a damn what happens now; it is all broken anyway." My tears started flowing uncontrollably.

"I know you never wanted me as your son!"

My hands grasped his throat. His eyes bulged with raw terror. "I'll kill you and finish you off!" I screamed again. "I don't give a shit anymore."

My strength, armed with righteousness, became a powerful weapon, while his horrified body was unable to react. "You are not leaving me, you God damned bastard." My words seemed to hit him in his face and I saw fear, real fear. My body was shaking as I came to an emotional end. I let go of him and sank, crying, to the floor. He only was able to say,

"OK, I will stay" and with that we passed through the coldest and loneliest Christmas ever.

From that moment on, the word 'father' left my vocabulary!

My situation here in the flat, the place I once called home, was unendurable and after a short time, he told me to leave. I stepped out of the field of broken dreams and moved into the uncertainty of ever changing lodgings.

The many beliefs I had for my future crushed in a single action by the man who supposedly should have helped me grow up.

Finish - Passé – It is over.

CHAPTER 19

My journey to becoming an adult

None of us would choose to be Sisyphus; yet in a sense, we all are

Joko Beck

Sisyphus *teaches us to never give in to circumstantial disappointments or try to escape from the failures, rather accept failures the same way we accept our achievements. And most importantly, no matter how much we lose in our quest, we must never back down until we fulfil our potential.*

With that one gesture from my father, I had entered onto the world stage of harsh reality, without the guiding hand of my mother or grandmother.

Kicked out of our family home, I looked for some affordable accommodation. My small amount of apprenticeship salary left no room for any luxurious dwelling. The vagabond life of looking for a cheap roof over my head had started. I rented small rooms let by lonely old people, mainly widows. In the first weeks after this shock, I cried many times. From whichever part of Hamburg I was living, I took the bus on many weekends to accept welcome food from my aunts (my grandma's sisters).

The old man (my father) still managed his small grocery shop. I had friends in that part of Hamburg and from time to time, I passed his shop. On one occasion, I was just walking by when he came out of the door. Without any fancy words he said, "Would you like to have your old room back? " He was never one for many words. "You can live here again."

I have no idea why I accepted his offer, but the reason must have been my financial situation, which had become a never-ending balancing act.

I nodded. "Yes, thanks, that will help. When do you want me to move in?" "Anytime you want. The room is empty as I am here alone," he answered, to my surprise.

After I was able to digest this announcement, I thought that something must have happened. Was the liaison with his woman friend finished? Did they have a row? Anyhow, I accepted. I cancelled my lodgings at the end of the month and organised my move back home.

It was a sunny weekend day when my friend came to pick me up. My only possession was a small bookcase, which we managed to get onto the backseat of his VW Beetle Cabriole. We stopped in front of the shop and unloaded the piece of furniture.

"Hey, hey, stop, stop what are you doing?" He shouted, running out of the door. "No, no, you can't live here; there is a change in the situation, it is impossible for you to have your room!"

I knew it, it was too good to be true, another kick in the backside from my old man. There was not one word of apology or explanation. Only unspoken words of, 'Piss off, you are not wanted here', hung in the air. Again, the usual disappointment repeated itself, I should have known better.

"But I have cancelled my rented room. I have nowhere to live. You cannot do that to me, not again. It is too much! Where will I go?" I had to bite my lips to keep my temper and fists in check.

After a long and sometimes noisy argument, he agreed to let me in, to have my former room, but only for a limited time. It does not require a great deal of imagination to see that our emotional and communicative capacities were incompatible. After this, hardly a word was spoken.

Easter arrived and I dreaded it, another festivity we usually enjoyed and celebrated in our family. However, my friend and band member Bernd knew about my plight and invited me to join his family during the festive days. It was a welcome change from the gloom of the past days.

After this, I could not cope with the situation anymore and moved out. I got information that there was some kind of a habitable room in a derelict house. Another of my friends drove me to my new home. The building stood in Hamburg Altona, at the northern end of the notorious Reeperbahn, Hamburg's red light district. The old two-storey house earmarked for demolition. Somehow, I found a way to make it my home for some weeks before I was evicted. The trail continued to find more rented rooms during the last years of my apprenticeship.

I had invitations from friends and their parents fed me from time to time. As before, I went on weekends to my aunts. They provided me with dinner and pocket money, which I greatly appreciated.

I started to go to some clubs to listen to Bill Haley and Chubby Checker and danced to the music of the Rolling Stones and others. However, I preferred jazz and went with some like-minded enthusiasts to many concerts in Hamburg's Music Hall. I was lucky enough to see The Count Basie Orchestra, Louis Armstrong, Ella Fitzgerald, Dave Brubeck, Oscar Peterson and many others. On Friday evenings, I went with some friends to Hamburg's fish market and listened to jazz bands in smoked filled rooms.

In the summer, there were jazz concerts in the City Park. The only problem was that we had to deal with rockers, trying to beat us up every time we congregated at the event.

My friends and the music helped me to clear my head and to overcome the anger I still had in me, over what the old man (my father) had done. Slowly I started to change from negative to positive thinking. My experiences enriched my new approach to life, and the psychological lessons I learned made me stronger.

Apart from working in the office, I also had to attend a business school once a week. After a three year apprenticeship, using the same plagiarism that had helped with my final school certificate, I managed to obtain a diploma, which would open the doors for my future in commerce.

However, as soon as I began to get comfortable and look forward to starting my commercial life and earning some money, somebody or something had different ideas.

It felt like, one step forward and two steps backwards.

CHAPTER 20

Your country needs you

Do your duty as you see it, and damn the consequences

George S. Patton Jr.

One day the postman presented me with a suspicious brown envelope. It would influence my future with marching steps. I had to undertake my eighteen months compulsory military service. There was no way around it.

The army doctors examined me and the other poor victims. Some tried to escape conscription by being medically unfit. We had to supply a urine sample, to make sure no diseases were lurking in our bodies that would exclude us from this heroic task. Some clever thinking would-be soldiers pricked their fingers and dripped blood into the sample, to simulate some internal illnesses. However, the eagle-eyed doctors had seen this before, and no one got away with this pretence.

I joined the German Border Troops, because they paid more money than the regular army. From the moment the ink of the recruiting officer's signature dried on my listing paper, the country was in safe hands. I still looked like a child, even though I was an official soldier. It gave me the advantage of being able to purchase a child's ticket on public transport.

The country could now sleep peacefully as I was an official West German border guard. My entrance into the German defence system started in the autumn of 1965 at a very eventful time. Fences and warning posts had been installed by East Germany in country areas, along the demarcation line between East and West Germany. Within weeks of my enlistment, we saw East German troops cutting down trees, establishing wide-open strips of bare land. Suddenly, they erected watchtowers, combined with a carpet of planted mines and used vicious dogs on kilometre long leads, to prevent and even kill anybody, trying to flee the glorious Socialist Republic of East Germany. Our troops were often called out when mines exploded. Only animals were the victims of this barbaric bulwark, in our section. The construction of these murderous barriers started four years after 1961, when the Communist government of the German Democratic Republic (East Germany) began to build a concrete 'Antifascism Security Wall' between East and West Berlin. We read in the newspaper and watched on TV people being shot at the Berlin Wall, in front of the eyes of the whole world.

Decorated with helmets designed in the Second World War we marched and crawled. After a particularly long and exhausting march, we took off our boots and socks in our dormitory, occupied by eight comrades, which created a very special aroma.

At our drill ground, we stood to attention and an eager sergeant screamed at us and tried to tell us what we had done wrong. After weeks of this senseless torture, we were apparently prepared for a so called 'war exercise.'

A long journey, on open trucks, took us to the place of action. It was an area of heathland and forest. As darkness descended, our sergeant major ordered us to the position we had to occupy with our machine guns and anti-tank mortars. Suddenly, there were explosions everywhere, and amidst all this, thirty or more large tanks started their engines. The noise deafened us and made the ground shake, as our machine guns fired at an invisible enemy in total darkness.

By chance, I turned around in this mayhem and saw a tank advancing in our direction. Realising the danger we were in, I jumped up, grabbed the machine gun, kicked my two mates and screamed, "Scheisse, raus, raus, raus, schnell schnell."(Shit, out, out, out, quick quick)

We jumped out of our shallow foxhole and leapt out of the path of this approaching monstrosity. Within seconds, a thirty-ton tank ran over our position. We stood frozen with open mouths, unable to speak, just staring at how its tracks had flattened the ground, in which we had just laid.

"Bloody Hell" was all we could utter.

(The third intervention from my guardian angel.)

We carried on playing soldiers, and marched and suffered through the remaining time.

On any free weekend, I drove back to Hamburg, as I was now in possession of an old VW Beetle.

Late one Saturday night, it was my turn to give some comrades a lift. We joined the motorway in Lübeck for our short trip to Hamburg. There were four of us in the car. Suddenly, I became aware of the approaching headlights of another vehicle. These lights came rapidly towards us and I then realised the car was on our side, driving on the wrong side of the motorway. At the last minute, I was able to yank the steering wheel to the left and skidded onto the hard shoulder while this potential murderer passed us at hundred kilometres an hour. After we stopped, we all got out of the car and sat on the grass, smoking well-needed cigarettes. If I had not reacted so quickly, there would have been now four dead bodies on the road.

(The fourth intervention of my guardian angel.)

Amongst all that marching and barrack duty, we experienced a comical event, well, at least for us suffering soldiers it was. It happened on a dull, damp autumn day. Colourful leaves floated gently onto the glistening asphalt at the entrance of our barracks, creating a slippery carpet. A new recruit, on his first sentry duty, walked up and down guarding the entrance. The wet and wintry breeze of mist and rain engulfed the surroundings, making it unpleasant for him, standing there in the drizzling rain. There was no reason to have the barrier down, because a soldier was on duty.

However, some meters behind him a chain, invisible in this weather, as extra security stretched across the road. The newcomer was well aware of the rules that anybody approaching had to show identity, before given permission to enter the barracks. He was cold and waited for his replacement, as he was nearing the end of his shift.

He turned around and stood at the barriers, as he heard a motorbike approaching. What he did not know, sitting on the bike was the Commanding Officer of our division, who never showed his identity pass.

He stepped into the road to fulfil his duty, but the rider passed him, disregarding the regulations. The sentry went to sound the alarm because of this unidentified intruder, when he heard an almighty crash.

The Commander in his black leather coat had crashed into the chain, which caught the bike, and he catapulted from his seat. He flew past the chain and landed in a heap on the grass strip, while his motorbike found its own way, past him. The poor recruit did not grasp the situation at all. He approached the Commanding Officer with a voice of authority, "Could I please see your identification?"

At that time, the perplexed biker stood up, steaming with anger, but had to control himself, as the new soldier had acted according to the rules. It was only then that the new recruit realised who he had in front of him.

After this incident, I never saw anybody made to clean toilets or march as much as this young man did.

For eighteen long months, I helped to foil any planned assault by the East Germany army and its Russian allies, upon our hard working Capitalist Nation. It was eighteen months of my life, where I was paid, not to think, but to obey. I left the military without any promotion, which usually was awarded to anyone, as long as they kept their nose clean.

Somehow, I must have forgotten to stick to the rules.

CHAPTER 21

Life can be crazy

We are all in the gutter, but some of us are looking at the stars
Oscar Wilde

After completing my duty of defending my country, I moved back into lodgings in Hamburg and started an office job for a delicatessen import company. We imported caviar, lobsters and exquisite food from all corners of the world. The added bonus was that we had to taste and approve samples before a deal was agreed. I tasted delicacies I never knew existed.

However, after a while I was bored out of my head and resigned. As music was my hobby, I decided to become a disc jockey and was hired by a high class night club in the centre of Hamburg. I met a number of rich and 'pseudo rich' people. Some of these posers were such liars that it became embarrassing to take them seriously. A new world of pretense and showmanship was presented to me. What a place to study humankind! When alcohol starts to take effect, it can unlock a chamber of secrets and it is fascinating what can be disclosed. Who needs to go to university to study psychology? I opened my ears and my mind and learned a lot about my fellow countrymen, hoping to use this knowledge on my way through life.

I rented a flat in an affluent area. It was the same flat in which my sister had started her married life. I was in seventh heaven after moving into my own little castle. The shadows of my turbulent family life slowly drifted away, but never quite left me.

During this time in Hamburg, I joined a bunch of guys in a skiffle group. We met as often as we could at 'Danny's Folk Club' where I started to play the washboard. It was 'IN' at that time to drink tea, and talk about art, music and have long hair. A lot of this was intellectual nonsense, which mostly went over my head. We listened to people like Donovan and Peter, Paul and Mary.

Hey, whatever I was part of it.

Many of this colourful group of hippies smoked some substances that were not acceptable in legal circles. One drug dependent smoke head had a Citroen 2CV known, as the 'Ugly Duckling. ' On some weekends, we drove in a convoy, loaded with barrels of beer and stronger stuff, to isolated beaches at the North Sea or The Baltic Sea. We erected our tents, started our campfire and tapped into the beer barrels. Out came the instruments and music enticed us to dance and sing. Clouds of ignited joints floated into the night sky. The slowly disappearing evening sun and diminishing beer and schnapps led us into our tents and sleeping bags. Some guys, intoxicated by drinks and drugs ended up in different tents, and enjoyed the comfort of whatever was on offer.

In the morning, our 'Ugly Duckling' driver organised a trip across the beach. He drove at quite some speed, steering his vehicle wildly from left to right. He screamed with delight whilst sucking frantically on his pipe loaded with weed. Suddenly, without any warning, he pulled the steering wheel around, the car groaned and crashed into the waves of the Baltic Sea. We passengers, still hungover and affected from the aromatic smell of his pipe, were killing ourselves with laughter and holding on for dear life. Our bawling and cheering only stopped as the Baltic's water entered the vehicle and it gave up the ghost with a last splutter. Our stoned driver yanked the door open and with arms outstretched, shouted, "I AM FREEEEEEE. I swim to Russia" and with this he jumped head first into the water. We all followed him running into the waves.

"Shit, the tide is coming in," was our alarming cry. Our 'Ugly Duckling 'did not oblige and its motor did not want to start. We tried now to push and drag the car out of the rising water. However, our driver was still splashing in the water without a worry in the world. Finally, we managed to free the car and get it started and drive back to the camp.

There was one more day and night of drinking, singing and much more. The fire was burning into the night and a barbecue was organised to satisfy our hunger. Next morning we packed up and my friend Gerd gave me a lift home in his shiny Alfa Romeo. Oh yes, I also had a rich friend.

Back home, I sat on my own and tried to take stock of my life so far. Did I want to lead a hippy life? I realised very quickly that this bunch of hippies were quite funny, but without the depth, I was looking for. Is that what I wanted, or did I want to take an office job in which I died of boredom? Of course, the army was not an option, as I had had sufficient experience in the eighteen months of my involvement.

My mind submerged in the emotions of this problem, and I was uncertain of an unknown future and of being alone, but I was not frightened. At this stage of my life, I had no idea what I wanted. I knew I wanted more; to see the world and break away from the direction my life had led me so far.

The only thing I knew for sure was that I would never be like my father.

CHAPTER 22

If you don't know where you are going, any road will take you there

You only live once, but if you do it right, once is enough

Mae West

My friend Paul, whom I knew from the scout days, still lived with his parents. After our days together at the boy scouts, our lives had gone in different ways but we kept in touch as friends. While I chose a commercial apprenticeship, he became a petrol station attendant. His workplace was in the city centre, below a building that would play a significant part in our lives.

One night Paul's father asked him if he would help him to collect some goods. Paul then asked me, if I was interested to help, as we would be paid.

Later that evening we drove with his father in a van, to a dress shop in the centre of Hamburg. Paul's father somehow unlocked the door (I do not know how) and switched the alarm system off. Then we started to empty the store completely of all its clothes. Whilst we were carrying dresses and other garments into the van, I started to wonder why we were doing this in darkness. It did not feel right and I felt like a thief on a raid. He must have realised my concern, because he looked at me and said,

"I only take back what I am owed, because these people have promised for three months to pay me, but have no intention to do so, and now my patience has come to an end."

He then put a twenty Mark note in my hand.

Paul told me his father had the sold the goods which we removed, previously to this customer,

I became uneasy about Paul's fathers personality and behaviour. There was more to him, then being an ordinary businessman. I had my suspicions and asked Paul about his father's business.

"I'm not quite sure what he is doing, but I don't ask questions and I would advise you to do the same, "was his advice.

I became aware, that Paul's father was not a man you could or should question, as I already had experienced some time ago, when I first started to smoke.

On that day, I called on Paul with a lit cigarette in my hand. It was my very first legal smoke and I felt grown-up. I rang the doorbell. His father opened the door. He looked at me and started laughing.

"What is this all about? Are you mad or just stupid?" With this, he lurched forward, snatched my cigarette and gave me an almighty smack.

"Got the message?" Still laughing he closed the door. Somehow, I did not get the message, as I carried on smoking. Just not, near him.

A week later Paul told me,

"I have chucked my job in and now have my own business and an office in the city."

I was perplexed, as this would have required a substantial amount of money, as well as long term planning.

"When did this happen?" I asked

"A month ago, you should come over one day and have a look. I might need some assistance. OK?" he offered.

"OK, I will," was my reply. I was curious to find out what business he was in and how he could afford or find the money to rent an office in the centre of Hamburg. Who was financing it? If I find out that his father is behind this enterprise, I will avoid any involvement like the plague.

However, his invitation started a chain reaction that words simply cannot describe. Events and incidents triggered situations, which would influence my life for a very long time to come.

Next day, I went to meet him. We met in a cafe in the Centre of Hamburg. He explained to me, that he was buying spare parts for all major car manufacturers. These were not the branded parts, but fully functional and ten times cheaper.

Whilst we were sitting having a coffee, a large, aggressive looking man joined us. Paul introduced him as Werner. After listening to their conversation, I became even more suspicious as to how Paul was able to build up this organisation from nothing. Was it with his father's help, who, as it later turned out, was a leading racketeer and mafia boss in Hamburg? On the other hand, maybe it was it this Werner, who looked like a very slippery character?

However, I concluded, who was I to ask?

After this meeting, Paul's as well as my own life went in an unimaginable direction. A couple of days later he again invited me to his office.

"What are you doing these days?" he asked.

"I am a DJ in a bar at a nightclub" I replied.

"Why don't you come and work with me?"

"I have not the slightest clue about spare parts or any other part of your business."

"It doesn't matter. You could come with me if I have to go and meet some people or come to the office and the rest we will see. OK?"

He was waiting for my answer.

"Look, if you say yes, I'll give you one hundred Mark now and invite you for dinner!"

"Yep, why not, as I have nothing else to do during the day."

"Great, business is booming and I will pay you some salary."

I put the hundred Mark note into my pocket and did not realise then, that my life's course had been set. I resigned from my job as a DJ, and dived into an unknown future.

The next morning I went to his office. It was located in the centre of Hamburg, based on the fourth floor of a modern building. His secretary was sitting in the reception room and with a smile, told me to go through. Paul sat behind a large desk. Without any long introduction or details, he said,

"Look, you are my assistant. When we go to see customers or dealers, you will be with me. OK?"

"What is my salary? I have to pay my rent and have to live."

"Don't you worry about anything; you will be OK and won't regret it."

It seemed details were not part of the arrangement.

"Gabi, come here and get us a drink, we have something to celebrate," he called to his secretary.

Gabi entered the room and opened a bottle of champagne,

"Let me introduce you to my friend, Rudi, he is working with us. Cheers to the future and success!"

She sat on Paul's desk bending over him, to show him that she was not only good at typing letters, but also had other assets.

I was amazed and surprised how quickly my life's path has changed, in a blink of an eyelid. One thing was certain, whatever I had let myself in for, this was not a normal commercial enterprise or organization. Another hundred-Mark note found its way into my pocket.

Confused, I went home.

CHAPTER 23

Light and shadow become blurred

The right to stupidity is a guarantee of the free development of the personality.

Unknown

It was a Friday evening and I was sitting in a pub on my own. A glass of beer was my only companion. The scenario of the last few days was swirling through my head. I tried to analyse what had happened, but could not make any sense of it. Why did my friend give me two hundred Mark, for which in the past I had to work a month to earn?

I ordered another glass of beer and more questions occupied my thoughts. Was Paul trying to pay for friendship, respect and blind submission? One thing was certain, money talks and can impress, if you let it, even if the person talks rubbish, as I found out during my time as a DJ. It is like watching a spider enticing its clueless victim into its net. Had I been caught in that net? Was I a victim? Would I be different from all the others he had tried to impress with his money? Maybe he was looking at me as a friend he could trust and rely on?

I was not sure. Time will tell, I thought.

I looked around, noticing all the other people in the pub. Office staff and factory workers had finished their work load for another week. They were being wedged into underground trains, trams and buses to make their way home. Then, they would repeat it over and over again, until retirement or death released them from that treadmill. I wanted more. I wanted out of this humdrum everyday life. I was hungry for adventure and travel. Maybe I was stupid to ignore any signs of lingering doubts, but I had nothing to lose.

Maybe it had something to do with the fact, that all those years ago, I had been sitting on that wall in front of our house feeling rejected and seeing friends departing with their parents, whilst I never enjoyed a family holiday. I finally I wanted to forget those tears of humiliation. I experienced the premonition that one day even the beautiful city of Hamburg might become too small for me. I wanted to grab life with both hands.

A few weeks later, I was having dinner with Paul in one of Hamburg's top restaurants, when he said,

"Why don't you cancel your flat and I'll organise more central accommodation for you. I'll pay for it as part of you working with me?"

"Are you sure?" I asked in amazement

"Yes, look I can afford it. Money is no object. I have an accountant who will put all these expenses through the company," he smiled.

He rented an apartment for me in a very sought after district. We went out most evenings to eat and my past life disappeared into a distant cloud of memories. Paul paid for every meal and the endless appearance of one hundred Mark notes left its impression on me. I moved into this fully furnished apartment and thought I was in heaven. After ten or more years in lodgings I now lived the dream.

One morning there was a knock on the door and Paul said,

"Get ready; we are driving to the office. Somebody is waiting for us."

As we went out of the front door, he moved towards a metallic blue car. I stood on the road as if struck by lightning.

"What the hell is that?" was all I could say.

"It's a Mercedes 500," he replied and with this, he clicked the fob and opened the door.

I did not ask any more questions. We were driving through the city and suddenly he took the receiver from the car phone, which I had not noticed.

"Gabi, is Werner already in the office?"

I was speechless, as I had never seen a phone in a car before.

We arrived at the office and I came face to face, with the man I had met there before. He was a most imposing figure.

"Heh, you are late, letting me wait here like an idiot!" his voice boomed. "Who the devil is this?"

His large finger pointed at me. He must have had forgotten that we had already met.

"This is Rudi, my new assistant."

Werner looked at me suspiciously, seemingly not happy with my involvement.

"Just relax, we've known each other for years and he will work with us," Paul said to calm him.

Was that a slip of the tongue? What did he mean 'with us?

"Listen, I'll meet you this evening in the club, OK?" It was not a request but a statement from Werner.

"OK, we'll see you there" Paul replied.

"Don't be bloody late again," he frowned.

He put an unlit cigarette between his lips and left the office. It seemed to me, that he was at the top of the pecking order. That evening we drove to a Members Only Club, and were greeted by an elegant woman in her forties.

"Nice to see you" she said, greeting Paul like an old friend, or 'client'?

"Inge, say hello to Rudi, he has just joined me"

A warm handshake and an inviting smile sealed the introduction. We settled in an exclusive, private room, where Werner was already waiting for us with a bottle of Champagne. He lit a cigarette and through a cloud of smoke, he said to Paul,

"I want to talk to you in private."

"Werner, listen to me. Rudi is an old friend of mine whom I totally trust. So, whatever you have to say, you can say it while he is present; OK?"

"Well, on your head be it "he said, not sounding convinced.

"Have you made a decision about joining me?"

"Yes, I am interested. The only thing is, we have to agree who is responsible for organising the legal aspect of forming a company, and who is handling the administrative and commercial side."

"OK, Paul your part is to establish the company, organise the export papers, packaging and shipment and I do the rest to secure the order." Werner suggested. "Is that OK with you? You have more experience and knowledge in dealing with this part of the business?"

They shook hands and with this a deal between them seemed agreed. After this meeting, we drove back to my apartment. We sat down and had a coffee.

"What is that deal?" I asked Paul.

"Does it matter?" was his short answer.

"Yes, please don't think I am an idiot. Now you have asked me to work with you, I want to know what is going on," I replied.

"OK; let's sit down and I will try to explain."

I made us a coffee and he started

"Werner has very strong contacts in an African country. That is what he told me. Either this or he works for the Secret Service, for which side I do not know, but I am aware he is quite often over there. He mentioned that he is now working on a large order for water pumps for an irrigation system at a new housing development, paid by the government. He wants me to help him to handle the export transaction so I am organising all the necessary documentation, packing and shipping. He will be responsible for all payment and distribution. Let us wait and see what happens. I will be in touch, as I might be busy for a couple of days."

He said goodbye and left.

I sat there and tried to take in what he had just said. I had a feeling that something was odd. Maybe I just was not used to or ready for any business, let alone big business. Maybe I was not comfortable with Werner's personality. I did not have an answer. Was this the gateway to the shadowy side of life? Did I have any evidence to dismiss Paul's offer as anything other than a big business opportunity?

No; was the answer.

CHAPTER 24

Diving into a crazy life

To live is the rarest thing in the world - most people only exist

Oscar Wilde

"Yes?" I shouted as somebody knocked on my door.

"It's me, Paul!" His voice sounded excited. I was in bed and half asleep, I opened the door.

"What, you are still sleeping? The sun is shining. It's such a beautiful day, just look out of the window. What can you see in front of the door?"

I could not believe my eyes. In front of the apartment, in the bright spring Hamburg sunshine stood a metallic green beach buggy. It had no roof, but shiny beige leather seats.

"What the heck is that? Is it yours?"

"Yep, I bought it yesterday. Come on, get your gear on and let's drive somewhere for a couple of days."

"Where do you want to go?" I asked.

"Don't know. Got any ideas?"

"Listen. I will come with you, but only if we make it special, crazy."

"OK. Where?"

"Let's drive to Sweden. I will come with you and only take a toothbrush and passport, nothing else and the same for you?" I suggested.

He replied, "That's a deal. Let's go."

And that was that. We jumped in the buggy and drove to Travemünde, the same ferry port; we had departed from, as fifteen-year old boys. The open top buggy, with tyres as wide as a tractor, was now occupied by two young men with long hair and not a piece of luggage. We thought we looked cool and it felt beautiful in the sunshine.

However, as soon as the sun disappeared we realised how cold it was as the wind whistled through our clothes. Paul ordered us a cabin for the crossing to Sweden. We arrived in Trelleborg, and drove off the boat towards passport control, stopping right under the sign:

'Welcome to Sweden'

A stern looking customs officer approached the buggy. "Passports, please; what is the purpose of your trip?"

"Holiday," we replied.

"And where are you going?"

"We don't know yet. Maybe we'll drive to Gothenburg or maybe to Stockholm."

"How long are you planning to stay in Sweden?"

"I think it will be a week or ten days," I replied

"Have you got enough money to pay for your stay?"

"Yes, we don't have a problem"

"Just wait here," he said, as he took our passports and disappeared into the office. After maybe fifteen minutes, he came back and said,

"Park your car over there, get out and wait in the room next to the office."

Sitting on a wooden bench next to a desk, we were nervous and anxious, although we knew we had nothing to fear. We stood by the window and watched two customs officers searching every inch of the buggy. First, they took the two seats out, and then they unscrewed the tyres and deflated them, including the spare.

"You know what, they think we are trying to smuggle drugs or alcohol," I told Paul. "Only because we don't look like your normal tourists with suitcases, they think we are criminals. That's why they don't want to waste any hot coffee on us, and let us sweat in this hole."

After approximately four hours, one of the officers came into the room and gave us the car keys and passports back. He did not look happy.

"Maybe you are smart and hiding something or you are just plain stupid to come to Sweden like this. Although we did not find anything, I can tell you, we will keep an eye on you and now bugger off."

Finally, we were on our way and arrived in Gothenburg. We were sitting in a café and letting the world go by. On another table, just opposite, we noticed four lovely blond Swedish girls, having a good time on this lovely spring afternoon. They seemed in good spirits, as they were talking excitedly, only interrupting themselves with loud laughs. They were about our age, and with their colourful dresses, they painted a beautiful picture.

"Do you see what I see?" said Paul and with that he was off to say hello.

He invited them over to our table and, of course, paid for their drinks. They were full of life, which I found extremely pleasing. My interest was drawn to one girl called Astrid. Her bright blue eyes and her shoulder length blond hair, framed a cheeky face, full of laughter and mischief. When these four girls came to our table, I made sure; I was sitting next to her. We conversed in English.

"What are you guys doing here in Gothenburg?" Astrid asked.

"We don't know yet. We've just arrived from Hamburg and want to stop over here for a day, before we drive on, maybe to Stockholm," I answered.

An hour later we went to a traditional Swedish restaurant where we had drinks, a beautiful dinner and stayed until early evening.

"Where will you stay?" one of them asked.

"We don't know; we have not booked anything," Paul replied. After some more drinks she said, "Why don't you come and stay with us?"

"OK, sounds good to me," he answered. It turned out they were all nurses in training and lived in accommodation at the hospital.

"Let's go. We will show you where we live, but you can only come in after dark, as we are not allowed to have any visitors, especially not boys," she smiled. "By the way, as you cannot come through the front door, we will show you where you can climb over the wall," she laughed loudly.

We entered their accommodation via a high wall and climbed in through a window. We had to be very quiet, but it was worth it as we had a night to remember.

Next morning we were out of that place before any security became aware of our presence and we decided not to drive all the way to Stockholm, as Astrid told me that somewhere between Gothenburg and Malmö, there was a music festival. What a wonderful idea. The only problem was, when we arrived at the event that it started to rain torrentially. We drove into town and bought some bin liners to use as raincoats and then drove on to the festival. The ground was saturated with mud and the rain formed small lakes. We were sitting in the buggy, waiting for the music to start and were shivering with cold. As we had no roof, water started to gather in the car. After we opened the doors to let the water out, we looked at each other and with one voice said,

"Sod this, we are out of here."

Never mind that we had just paid the £80 entrance fee. With teeth chattering and freezing cold, we drove back to the ferry port in Trelleborg.

Back in Hamburg, I was confined to bed for two weeks with a stinking cold. Paul came to visit me after I recovered from my illness. He never waited for any invitations, no, that was not his style. He sat down and without asking how I was, said,

"Werner has a government contract for the water pumps for an irrigation system. I can't use my company to complete the deal. Therefore, we have decided we need to open a new company, not in Hamburg, but in another big city. Listen, you will go and live in Munich for a while and I will tell you when and under what name to form and register a company there. OK?"

I said nothing, but just looked at him waiting for more information.

"You travel to Munich and stay in a hotel until you find an apartment in the city centre. I will pay for everything; all your travel, rent and you'll get enough to live on and make some good friends. Now, have a good time and enjoy your stay. Agreed?"

No argument or questions from me. I only said,

"Agreed!"

We shook hands and that was that.

"Now, before you leave, let's have a good time in Hamburg."

We went to his favourite restaurant and he ordered some caviar and we washed it down with a bottle of Champagne.

"What are you celebrating?" I asked.

"Nothing, I just feel like it."

After dinner he said, "Here is one hundred Mark, take a taxi home and I will see you tomorrow afternoon."

I went back to my apartment. I walked up the stairs and heard some noise, which I thought was coming from my flat. When

I got up the stairs, I saw a young lady searching in her handbag for the keys to next door.

"Can I help you?" I asked

"No thank you it's OK. I'm looking for the keys I just collected from the estate agent," she smiled.

"If you are moving in here, then we are neighbours. I am Rudi," I introduced myself and we shook hands.

"Sophie," she replied in a south German accent.

"Nice to meet you! I am sure we will meet again and if you need anything, just knock on my door."

"Thanks," and with this she disappeared into her apartment.

She was an elegant young girl, very beautifully dressed. I guessed she must have been fifteen or sixteen years old. I was wondering, how such a young girl could afford the rent in such an expensive part of Hamburg.

Next day, in the afternoon, Paul came to see me. He opened the door with his own key, which he thought was acceptable, as he paid the rent. I told him about the very young, attractive looking girl who had moved in yesterday evening. He got more excited than I had seen him before. After I tried to describe her he said,

"Go, knock on her door and see if she needs anything, and then introduce me."

Ten minutes later the three of us were sitting in my flat chatting. Then Paul, in an effort to impress, invited her for dinner with us at his special restaurant. Within days they became an item. He saw her every day and found out that she came from the south of Germany and was enrolled in a private school in Hamburg. Her parents were extremely rich and owned a well-known company.

She was only just fifteen years old.

After a few more weeks of living the high life in Hamburg I went to Munich as agreed. I found a flat in the city centre and started to make friends. Soon, I was introduced to a circle of people with money, businesses and large houses. I was invited to some parties and pub crawls, and we all met up on a Sunday morning at a pub. There was always a band playing and the atmosphere felt crazy. We were singing, dancing and drinking as if there were no tomorrow. I invited all my new friends, the band, and anybody who said hello to me to join in. It is a tradition in Germany that one pays one's bar tab at the end of the session, and all the drinks I had ordered were marked on my beer mats. After the band finished and it was time to go home, the barman tallied up my drinks. I was well drunk and did not feel the pain when he announced;

"Rudi, thanks for the great morning. We are closing now and your bill is ONE THOUSAND SIX HUNDRED and EIGHTY FIVE Mark."

I swallowed hard, but then remembered that all the money was provided and my accommodation sorted. The sun was shining and I felt as if I was in a dream.

After that Sunday morning I received more invitations. I was sitting in a pub in the old part of Munich, enjoying the special beer that's only brewed in Munich. Volker, one of my new friends, came in and we had a drink together.

"Rudi, Anette, who has a big house in the posh part of town, is having a party on the weekend. I told her about you and she has asked me to invite you. Are you free next Saturday?"

"Sure, no problem, I look forward to it, and please say thank you to her for inviting me."

"OK, will do. I'll pick you up around eight and we'll drive to her house."

Saturday came and became a day I would not forget in a hurry. Volker collected me and we drove to Anette's place. It was a large villa, nestled between well-trimmed hedges. A long walkway of white pebble stones, winding between some beautiful sculptures, and a carefully cultivated lawn ended at a very imposing solid wooden front door. Volker rang the bell and an attractive lady in her mid-thirties opened the door. She wore an elegant black dress, with a quite revealing décolletage.

"Hi, welcome," she kissed Volker and turned to me. "I'm Anette," she said offering her hand, which I took.

"Rudi," I replied.

"Nice to meet you, I am glad you could come, as I have heard a lot about you," she smiled." Come in, have a drink and meet the others."

The villa and its contents smelled of money. There were paintings on the walls, and expensive furniture and luxurious rugs in most of the rooms. I smiled and thought, I can get used to this lifestyle, first in Hamburg and now here.

The whisky and wine were flowing, slowly lowering the level of intellectual conversation. There was also a sweet smelling aroma in the air and some of the guests started to act in peculiar ways. People started to dance and I noticed an atmosphere of sexual intensity filling the room. The excess of alcohol encouraged couples to be more adventurous. Suddenly the first items of clothing were landing on the floor. Other guests followed and within minutes couples were rolling on the expensive rugs, completely naked. This was the start of an orgy, with no taboos, as nobody held back.

Suddenly, during these sexual gymnastics, we heard the door bell ringing. Without a second of hesitation, Anette went to open the door in all her naked glory.

"Taxi for......," the only words the driver managed to utter. His eyes nearly popped out of his head and his mouth stayed wide open in surprise, amazement or shock.

Anette smiled at him. "Come in, they are not ready yet," she said to the driver laughing loudly, as he looked intensely into the room. "You can wait here,"

With this she took him by the hand, led him in to the house and closed the door. Within a short while the taxi driver had joined the party and finished his nightshift in a way he had surely not anticipated

I just hoped he had not left his motor and meter running.

CHAPTER 25

A deal of a lifetime with consequences

At the most important crossroads of life, there are no signposts

Ernest Hemingway

Paul phoned me one day and said, "We are now ready to form the company. We are registering the following company name: 'INTERNATIONAL EXPORT GR0UP' as Werner has been advised by the Minister in charge. He is now in Africa, working with their government departments. The company will be formed in Munich with Werner and I registered as directors."

After the formalities of the registration and the receipt of the legal company documents, I left Munich and returned to my apartment in Hamburg. Paul still kept the apartment in Munich as the registered company address.

The high life with Paul continued and the champagne kept flowing. As a matter of fact, his antics to impress everybody increased.

It wasn't long, before Paul announced the news.

"Listen, Sophie and I are getting married," he smiled

"What? She is only young, I guess fifteen, are you crazy? How the hell will you do that? How will you marry her? Have her parents given their permission?" I asked.

He did not answer, but said, "Look, we will be away for some days and I will contact you when I am back."

I stood there with my mouth wide open and could not believe what I just heard. He was a twenty three year old man, who had been married before and now marrying a fifteen year old girl, against the will of her parents, and I think against German law.

Later, I found out they went to Scotland and got married in Gretna Green. Her father had warned her that if she went ahead and married 'this idiot' she would be struck off any inheritance. Apparently, she would only receive a one off payment of one million Mark and would have no more contact with her family.

Wherever we went he introduced his child bride like a trophy. He was known in all the expensive restaurants, and was always welcomed with great fuss.

"Good evening Sir," was the start of a very costly evening, as the Dom Perignon appeared, even before an order was given. A generous tip was awarded to the waiters for all their (over the top) attention. I must admit, that even I felt like a celebrity, being part of this show.

That there might be some dark clouds gathering in the future, and this fairytale story might end with an unpleasant outcome, did not occupy my mind. If I smelt a rat, I did not want to know. The present dream was too exciting.

A couple of days later Paul came to see me.

"Listen, you know I was married before, well, now my ex-wife is making a lot of noise, wanting some financial settlement. I have typed a certain statement, relating to my finances, but used the name of another person, to confirm my financial situation. I need you to sign as witness to confirm that this named person has written the statement."

"You must me joking, how can I sign the document? No, no I'm not signing it that can't be right. No way will I be part of it," I said, holding his gaze.

I notice he was really pissed off with me, but he accepted my refusal.

*

On that weekend, there was a knock on the door. I opened it and there he was.

"What the hell has happened to you?" I asked and started screaming with laughter, as I realised that he had dyed his hair black.

"Let's drive to Sweden, today. I want to spend some more time in Stockholm."

I just could not answer as my breath was taken away with laughter.

"I have dyed my hair, because the blonde girls in Sweden are hot for darker looking men. Get ready and pack some things. I will pick you up in the afternoon."

I was speechless in amazement and couldn't stop laughing. Quite honestly, I was at a point where nothing surprised me about him anymore. To say he was unique might be an understatement. As promised, he came back to collect me and we went outside.

"Where is your car?" I asked

"Over there" he replied and walked towards a brand new Porsche Carrera.

"I got it yesterday and thought we might take it on a trip," he said.

Before I could ask any questions, we drove to the ferry.

Arriving in Sweden, we drove all the way to Sodertalje, south of Stockholm. We checked into a motel and met the band Manfred Mann, who had some gigs around Stockholm. We found the famous night club 'Alexandra' in the city centre, where we spent nearly every evening.

(Alexandra disco was a well-known nightclub in Stockholm at the end of 70s and in the 80s. The photo sessions for Abba's 1979 album 'Voulez-Vous' took place there)

As usual, Paul let the champagne flow and did his best to impress the girls. However, even with his large investment in drinks and his dyed hair, the success rate was, zero.

On our way back to the ferry port Trelleborg, a police car chased us because we were travelling at double the legal speed limit. Fortunately, we escaped. Paul drove into a forest area, out of sight from the police, where we hid for some hours. I am sure, that we would have been heavily fined, or had to spend some time in government accommodation if they had caught us.

After our return to Hamburg, I would have liked to be a fly on the wall, when he tried to explain to Sophie why he had dyed his hair. However, knowing how he was able to persuade people to believe what he wanted them to, I am sure he found a way, as he had full control over her.

He also told me that her father, who had now disowned her, kept his word and had paid her one million Mark, as promised. He mentioned that they now have a shared bank account, which did not surprise me at all. I did not see him for a few weeks, as he spent most of the time with his young bride.

One day he appeared and had some news.

"Werner just called and told me that the consignment of water pumps for the irrigation systems have arrived in Africa and have been inspected and accepted. The government has authorised and released the payment. I have opened a bank account and the payment is now deposited."

I'd never seen Paul looking so intense, hyped up and excited.

"Werner was responsible for all the dealings with the African side. I have organized everything else here in Hamburg, and you helped to form the company in Munich. I will pay all parties involved; so far so good? Because Werner has to pay commission in cash to his people in Africa, I have decided that all of us will be paid in cash. As it was quite a large and important deal you will receive one hundred thousand Mark."

I looked at him in disbelief! I had to let this news sink in, in order not to faint. These numbers were circling in my head.

"Now, you and I are going to collect the money. I have made an appointment with the bank for Monday. OK?"

"How much are you talking about?" I asked.

"Two million Mark," was his short answer.

"Say it again."

"Two million Mark," he repeated. "I will pick you up on Monday afternoon, as our appointment is at six o'clock,"

With that he left. I spent the weekend digesting what had happened. It goes without saying that I could not sleep the night before Monday.

Monday arrived and so did Paul.

"Here, I have two Samsonite suitcases. Each of us will take one, in which one million Mark will be put. I have agreed that we can park the car directly in front of the bank."

I nodded.

"Ah, one cannot be too careful, thieves can be everywhere," he smiled.

I thought it sounded sarcastic.

"Therefore we will each carry a loaded pistol, just in case. You can tuck it in your belt. I have worked too long and hard to let any idiots rob us."

He handed me a nine millimeter revolver.

"You've been in the army and know how to use that thing. Listen, this is the end of the deal. We can go our own ways and you can do whatever you want with your share. Just think what this could mean for you. You might not get another chance like this. Now, when we arrive at the bank, don't look around and no suspicious behaviour. You will wait in the car, as I will conclude the deal with the manager. When you see me coming out of the door, you come and join me and we will load the suitcases into the car. The bank manager will wait at the door until we have disappeared. After this, we drive to my old apartment and you'll get your share of the deal. If all goes well, we will open a bottle of Dom Perignon, which is already cooling and waiting for us. Good luck!"

He looked at me to make sure I understood the enormity of his statements.

Later that afternoon we were sitting in the car with pistols sandwiched between our legs and two suitcases in the boot, which we hoped to fill with two million Deutsch Mark. As we approached the bank, Paul phoned the manager.

"We will be with you in five minutes," he said.

Of course, normally the branch would be closed for business at this time. Was I suspicious, maybe?

We arrived at the branch, and a man about fifty unlocked the door. His anxious face reflected his unease. His nervous body language revealed his thinking, 'I hope that this transaction will be dealt with rapidly'.

"Change of plan, you come with me into the bank," Paul said to me.

The bank manager greeted Paul with a weak handshake. Inside, Paul turned to me and said,

"You go into the other room, as I have to talk to him on my own."

Without any question, I moved into an adjacent room and waited. I did not know why but as I was on my own, I checked my pistol. After fifteen minutes, Paul came into the room.

"All is OK, come with me."

We went into the other office and my eyes popped out of my head. In the middle of the table lay a heap of bank notes.

"You don't have to count it," I heard the manager say, "It was all done automatically."

We stacked the notes into the two suitcases, and click - click, locked them immediately. The bank manager's face was now glistening with beads of sweat. The whole transaction had not lasted longer than thirty minutes and we were out of the branch. Both carrying a suitcase, containing one million Mark, loaded guns in our pockets. Once all was stowed in the car, we were off. I leant back in the seat and felt like a commercial robber. I still did not understand why an international export business had to end in such a dubious way, collecting all this revenue in cash.

What happened after this could be described as a release of stress and anxiety. We were reeling in a state of euphoria and I forgot any concerns I had about this business. Paul parked the car in front of his old flat, which I had only visited once, a long time ago. It was at a time when he was still happily married to his first wife.

He walked up the stairs, opened the door and deposited the two suitcases in the middle of the room. He opened both and without a word, started to throw the two million Mark in the air. It felt, like being in a film, unreal, as if manna was falling from heaven. Like two idiots possessed by the devil, we danced in this shower of money. After this performance, we gathered up all the notes and Paul counted out my share of one hundred thousand Mark.

"Here's your part," he said and then drove me home. "I'll call you."

Suddenly, money was not a worry anymore. My problem was that there was nobody who could advise me what to do with such wealth. I now reflect on what an idiot I was at that time by going into my local pub and trying to impress people by paying for my drinks with large bank notes. I now realise what a confused mental state I was in. To put it bluntly, I was lost and on my own, swept away into a world I did not come from, did not belong to and had no idea how to behave in.

Some days later, my doorbell rang and Paul's figure appeared in the door's spyhole. Since I was loaded with this large amount of cash, I had become more careful, with visitors.

"Have you got your passport ready?" he asked

"Why?" I really did not know why I bothered to ask questions anymore.

"Do you fancy flying to London? I have never been to England. I think it would be cool to get out of Hamburg for a while. Are you coming?"

It took me only a second and I started to pack my things. We jumped in a taxi to go to the airport. In London, we checked into the Hilton at Park Lane, where we stayed for two weeks. Sightseeing and expensive restaurants were our staple diet, until we flew back home.

What we were not aware of, was that dark clouds were gathering on the horizon of our future.

CHAPTER 26

At the end, every debt has to be paid

We are what we pretend to be, so we must be careful about what we pretend to be

Kurt Vonnegut

Deep in my mind, I had my worries that this international export deal was not a proper business transaction. However, it was too late to change it. I went along with every explanation I was given. I was hiding behind a mask, and I wore it for my own benefit. I pretended that I belonged to a circle of rich and powerful people. However, it soon became apparent, that I had been drip fed information that did not show the whole picture.

Early one morning, after a heavy night in my local pub, I heard loud knocking on my door. I was still in bed and not completely awake.

"Police, open the door."

I got out of bed, opened the door, and immediately surrounded by five police officers. They asked for my name, but I could only answer, "Sorry I have to rinse my mouth, as it is full of glass," I announced. They looked at me in amazement, as if I had just stepped onto this planet. The problem was, the aftermath of the speed tablets that I had taken in the pub the previous night, still affected me.

I dressed and they took me to the Special Fraud Squad headquarters. It was ironically located in exactly the same building where Paul had started as a petrol station attendant many years ago.

Two 'Special Fraud' officers, working for the German Inland Revenue, led me into a small room. I was cautioned, and told during my interrogation that a business had been established, in order to defraud the Inland Revenue of two million Mark of VAT payments.

I did not answer, and told them that I was waiting for my solicitor. After he arrived, the interrogators informed me, there were ten massive wooden cases, each with a dimension of four by four metres, each loaded with a small, used car motor. These cases had been delivered on open railway wagons to the port, for shipment to an African country. Apparently, unknown to anybody involved, the railway company filmed the complete process of the shipment.

My first day of interviews ended after eight hours.

I asked, "Am I arrested?"

"No, you are under caution. However, you have to be here every day at nine in the morning. Should you decide not to attend; an arrest warrant will be issued. Do you understand?"

"Yes, sir."

After I left the building, I called Paul immediately and told him what had happened.

"Shit. Listen, go to my father's and I will meet you there. OK?"

I made my way to his father's well-secured office. I rang the bell and his minder opened the door. "Wait here!" he said before letting me in.

"Where is Paul? He told me to come here?" I asked in surprise.

"You are stupid idiots!" Paul's father shouted at me. "How can you be so naïve and use the phone, after you knew the police were after all of you? Did it not occur to you arseholes that they are looking for Paul too? He came here but unknown to me; the police were already waiting for him. They arrested him and took him away in an unmarked car. I have no clue where they took him."

He was completely pissed off. I left the office before Paul's father resorted to violence, because he was shaking with anger.

The interrogation went on for nearly two weeks with up to six hours of questions a day. After my last interview, my solicitor informed me that everybody connected with this deal including the bank manager had been arrested or had an arrest warrant issued. I was the only one who not charged, as the interrogators realised that I had no knowledge this was an illegal business to defraud the Inland Revenue.

I heard nothing for weeks from Paul, his wife Sophie or his father. Apparently, nobody had any news of his whereabouts. Ten days later around midnight, I got a call.

"It's me." I immediately recognised his voice.

"Where are you? Everybody is worried like hell."

"Go to my father, he will tell you. I'll call you some other time."

"Are you OK?"

Yes" was his short reply and he hung up. Next day I went to visit his father. His minder opened the door again, but this time I went straight in.

"Well, any news?" His father asked me.

"Paul called and asked me to come and see you."

"I know," he replied. "So, apparently you are good friends and you don't know what is going on?" He shook his head and pointed to a chair.

"Sit down," he commanded. "Two weeks ago he made contact with me. He told me exactly what business he was involved in and he wanted some advice. I know he is in

Switzerland," he continued. "Max, bring us a soft drink," he shouted to his minder. "He then got in touch with me from Switzerland. I had a secure phone line and he told me how he was able to escape."

The drink came. After Max closed the door, he continued:

"Paul was put on the back seat of the unmarked police car. They came to a halt, at a traffic light, waiting in between other cars. He saw an opportunity to get away. I don't know why, but these idiots forgot to lock the back door." He laughed. "Anyway, the traffic lights changed and they started driving. He jumped out of the moving car and ran away. They never found him." He smiled. "He realised they had an arrest warrant. He knew he would have had problems getting out of the country. He had to organise things himself, before he could leave. He made his way to Leipzig, in East Germany, as he knew there would be no border control from West to East. From there he made his way to Zürich."

He looked at me, as if he was proud of Paul.

"By the way, his wife has followed him and is also now in Switzerland. I had no idea he was married again. Let's keep in touch, because I think he wants to contact you."

He even shook hands with me, for the first time.

The whole thing had become a nightmare and frightened me. I walked home. I felt an overwhelming sensation like a drowning man must experience, clinging on to a small plank in a rising flood, hoping to reach safety. Although money was suddenly no problem anymore, it felt as if this wealth was a burden hanging like a noose around my neck.

I left this illusionary world and dived straight into the murky surroundings of gambling, low life and drink. I entered a casino near the central railway station. After some initial games, I started to hold the bank, against all the other players. I took some speed tablets to stay wake and within hours, I had lost fifteen thousand Mark and was running out of money. I wanted to recoup some of my losses and called Paul's father.

"Could you lend me ten thousand?" I asked him.

"When do you need it?" he asked

"Now, I am in deep shit"

"Where are you?"

"I'm in a casino, holding the bank."

He started laughing aloud. "You are an idiot. Do you realise it's nearly midnight? OK, Max will bring it to you. When will you pay me back?"

"Within in three days," I replied.

"OK, three days and you pay me twelve thousand back."

After his minder delivered the money, it took me until the early hours to lose the lot. I asked the casino to give me some taxi money, and went home.

Did my fellow gamblers view me as an easy victim? I am sure. They all must have had a good laugh, and rightly, so, as an idiot like me does not come along every day. Maybe, it was my intention to offer myself as a victim.

I might have realised that the money I was gambling with was dirty, and I did not give a shit when it had gone or who benefitted from it. Three days later, I repaid the twelve thousand Mark from the stash I was hiding in my apartment.

The irony of borrowing money from Paul's father was that he was also a gambler. Only some days later, he went with his minder to an international casino and lost one million Mark.

After this loss, he banned himself from all the casinos where he had a membership. After this devastating loss, he returned to his office and had a massive argument with Max, his minder. During this confrontation, he lost control; took his revolver from his desk and shot him six times. Max died in his office and Paul's father went to prison on remand for some time. Somehow, he received a limited prison sentence, based on self-defence.

I started drifting from one bar to the other and realised soon that my life was going downhill fast and my drinking was getting out of control. I had a feeling, as if I was sinking.

I knew I had to change, before it was too late.

CHAPTER 27

I change my environment, but will it change me?

Though nobody can go back and make a new beginning... Anyone can start over and make a new ending

Chico Xavier

I had had enough. I was angry and on the verge of depression. Hamburg had become a dark place with its memories. There was nothing holding me back. I had to leave. I called a disc jockey agent and got a gig in a popular pub in a small industrial town. One week later, I took the train and was greeted on arrival by the landlord, Horst. The first week of my gig was a complete flop, as I could not connect with the guests. Horst said,

"Sorry, but it is not working. I will have to let you go. However, could you sit in this Saturday night, as the new guy is not available?"

"OK, no problem, I am waiting for my agent to relocate me," I replied.

Well, that Saturday I forgot the dark clouds of the past, and thought I would show Horst that I was capable of entertaining his guests. I was on top form and no guest left before two o'clock in the morning.

"Listen, you were great; if you want, I will cancel the other DJ and you can stay here!" He waited for my answer.

"OK, let's give it a go," I replied.

Something had clicked between us. We became very close friends and developed a strong partnership. After that crazy night, the guests accepted me. The word spread that there was a new DJ in town. I became so popular that I never had to pay for a drink in any other pub. Most of the local police force became friends and celebrated with us, therefore, we did not have to worry about licensing hours.

We had heard that a Hell's Angels gang was terrorising some towns and villages around us. One very busy evening they came into our pub.

My mixing decks were located at the end of the bar and one drunken guy started shouting, swearing, and tried to grab my micophone. I turned around and warned him a couple of times to stop. As he got louder and more aggressive, I swung around and pushed him away.

Very quickly I realised he was the leader of the gang. Suddenly, all hell broke loose and we were involved in the most vicious of fights. It got so dangerous, that Horst brought his Rottweiler into the pub. It only took five minutes for the dog to calm things down. By then most of the guests had left, as it was total mayhem and there was blood on the walls and on the bar.

Next day the leader and two of his mates came to see us.

"Listen, we are coming to kill your dog," he said, showing a long knife, concealed in his boot.

"OK," Horst replied, "You think you are such a big man? By the way, his name is Dux, so you know whom you want to kill. The dog remains next to me. I will not lead him to you, like a lamb to the slaughter. Go ahead, kill him!"

It was a very tense atmosphere, with an eerie silence. Horst sat in his chair, Dux next to him. I sat opposite. The guy's mind was working overtime, as he realised he couldn't back down in front of his mates. Suddenly, he leapt forward, pulling out the knife from his boot to kill the dog. Without Horst saying or visibly doing anything, eighty kilos of muscle flew through the air and had the chap pinned to the floor. Only Horst's command stopped Dux finishing him off.

Horst said very calmly, "Now you have two choices, either you never come back into my pub, or be civilised and shake hands. It's your shout."

He and his mates stood up and shook hands with us. After that, the Hell's Angels gang all behaved and became regulars.

My entertainment contributed, to the pub becoming the social centre of the town and hosting many memorable evenings. Over the next year, I became part of the local community.

Meanwhile, I was the proud owner of a blue Fiat 1500 and made many excursions with friends into the countryside. On some sunny days, we went to the nearby lake. One night, a group of us went skinny-dipping. I swam to the centre of the lake. When I returned everybody had disappeared, including all my clothes. After shouting for some help, I realised, they had played a prank on me. As far as they were concerned, it was successful. I had to walk naked to my flat, hiding in the dark between alleyways and bushes.

On a sunny afternoon, I decided to drive to another town. The only problem was, I already had had a skin full and was quite drunk. My car was parked in front of a lamppost at the market square. I started the car and wanted to drive off, but I could not find the reverse gear. Instead, I went forward and hit the post a number of times. Suddenly, there was a knock on my car window. Two police officers opened my door. They were regulars in our pub .

"What the hell are you doing? "

"I want to drive to the next village" I replied.

"Listen, you've had a drink. Don't be an idiot, get out and go home, OK?"

I nodded, locked the car and went round the corner. As soon as the two were out of sight, I went back, started the car and drove off. After five hundred metres, I had to stop at a traffic light. Without warning, a police car stopped in front of me, blocking my way. My two police mates came to my car, opened the door and with it, I fell out, flat on the tarmac. One of them helped me up and put me on the back seat of the police car. The other jumped in my car and followed. They drove me home, put me to bed and kept my car key. The next evening both came to the pub.

"Heh, Rudi are you feeling better?" they smiled "What do you think; shall we have a bottle of vodka?"

"That sounds good to me," I answered.

I took some breaks from the pub and got gigs in the Black Forest area and other cities in Germany. However, I always went back to Horst and got a warm welcome.

During my gigs, I met another DJ, who was completely crazy. He had heard about a still unknown, up and coming singer and managed to get hold of his demo record. He got a gig in a club in Bavaria and asked me to come with him. The idea was that he would pretend to be the singer, miming the song, while I played the record. We advertised the event and people had to pay an entrance fee. It all went well, until the record stuck and our ruse discovered. The audience chased us out of the club. Of course, it goes without saying, we were not paid, but we did get away without any lasting injuries.

On one occasion, I got a gig in small town pub an hour's drive from Horst's place. The proprietor was happy with a very successful night and we sat down and finished a bottle of brandy together.

"Are you OK driving back?" he asked

"Yes, no problem. It's not far, only through country side".

I said good-bye and got into my car. My car radio was playing and I was happy and singing, after a successful night. The road was straight and I increased my speed. Suddenly, without a moment to react, I drove into dense fog with hardly any visibility. At the only bend in this long stretch of straight road, I lost control and hit a roadside cement post, which the police later found in a field twenty metres away. My car crashed and somersaulted five times, and ended up on its roof in the adjacent field. I was lying squashed inside, hardly able to move. After I recovered my senses, I started kicking in the back window and crawled out. I looked at the flattened car and realised, how lucky I was to be alive. The most remarkable thing was, I only had a hole in my jacket.

(The fifth intervention of my guardian angel.)

It was pitch black and in the middle of nowhere, and there I was sitting on the grass, analysing what had just happened. There was no traffic. Then I saw some lights coming towards me. I walked into the road, stopping a car. A man, dressed as if he had just come from a function, climbed out of the car.

"Could you please help me and call my friend? I have just had an accident and I need him to pick me up," I pleaded.

"Are you alright?" he asked. Then he said, "I'm sorry I am not able to call him. I am the local police chief and as I am off duty, I will ask my colleagues to come and attend to you. My God, your car looks terrible. Was anybody else in the car, anybody injured or worse?" he asked.

"No, it is only me," I answered.

"Well, you were very lucky. I will inform them immediately, it should not take long."

After he drove off, I thought, thank God he did not notice that I was drunk. Afterwards I thought, he might have come from a function and had a drink himself. Maybe that was the reason why he did not asked me. I sat back on the verge and started eating grass because I thought that might disguise the smell of alcohol.

After about thirty minutes, two police officers arrived. I knew one of them.

"Jesus, your car, completely flattened!" He seemed shocked. "Is there anybody still inside; has anybody been injured or killed?" He asked with great concern.

I shook my head and then I started shaking like a leaf. "No, it is just me. Please give me a cigarette," and I pretended to cry to distract him from asking further questions. I lit the cigarette, puffed like a chimney, and asked for another one, while they took notes. They never asked me if I had had a drink. It was a lucky escape.

"We will call Horst and ask him to collect you. We know him well and have his phone number."

Horst came some hours later and the next day we removed the car from the scene. The negative thing about this episode was that I had to pay fifty Mark for the replacement of the concrete post that I had knocked over, and my car was scrapped.

Some weeks later Horst and I were sitting in his home discussing a business partnership.

"Last month I was in Lanzarote, in the Canary Islands. It is an up and coming tourist destination. I had a good look around and found a piece of land by the coast, with planning permission for a small hotel. Would you be interested in investing?" he asked me

"How much are we talking about?"

"We need sixty thousand Mark to purchase the land. If you are interested, you could contribute fifty thousand. I will contribute the ten thousand and pay for the construction costs. We could fly to Lanzarote next week so you can see the plot of land, before you make your decision, OK?"

"Sounds good to me," I replied.

The following week we went to inspect the plot and spoke to the sales agent. All looked good, and Horst and I agreed to go ahead with the deal. I gave Horst the required fifty thousand Mark and he went back to Lanzarote to conclude the deal. When he came back, we made plans regarding the legal and administrative side, to get the necessary documentation, to start the construction.

After two months, Horst came to see me. He put a newspaper down in front of me and I read the headline, 'International property fraud in Lanzarote exposed.' I was not sure if I wanted to laugh or cry. I had gained this money because of a fraud, and had now lost it because of a fraud. My financial gain from my involvement with Paul went full circle, first the loss in the casino in Hamburg, now the loss in a property fraud. I called Paul in Switzerland and told him about it.

"Never mind, I will look after you, I wanted to call you anyway. My father has arranged a party here in Zürich to celebrate my wedding anniversary. I want you to be here with me, as I always wanted you to be my best man."

I started to realise, that our relationship, as far as he was concerned was not only based on business. I was sure he regarded me as his friend. Maybe I was his best and only real friend.

"Can you come next week? I will send you a ticket."

"OK', I'll be there," I replied.

I told Horst to hire another disc jockey because I had to leave and was not sure, when I would be back. Although I stayed in contact with Horst and visited him from time to time, I never went back to work as a disc jockey in Germany.

Paul greeted me at Zürich airport. He was in a good mood and for the first time in a very long while, I saw him smiling again.

"You can stay with us. We have an apartment near Zürich and Sophie is looking forward to seeing you again. What are your plans?" he asked me.

"I really don't know. My money is more or less gone. I might go back to Germany and carry on as a DJ. What else can I do?" I asked.

"Forget all that shit. Let us have a good time and celebrate my wedding anniversary. You will be OK, I promise you," and with this we went to his car.

I stood in front of a blue Silver Shadow Rolls Royce. Somehow I was not surprised, just amazed at how he did all this. While we drove to his place, he started to open up.

"You know, when I asked you to meet me at my father's office, I was arrested, but managed to escape. I then took a train to Leipzig and then on to Switzerland." He started laughing, "It was not easy to make the journey with a load of hidden cash. It all became crazy. Think about it, I made one and half million from the deal, plus Sophie's settlement from her family. Suddenly I had two and half million Mark. By the way, I could not tell you the truth about the actual deal at the time, when I asked you to register the company in Munich. It was better for you that you were not in the picture."

It sounded like he had wanted to protect me from the truth and was apologising which I never heard him do before.

"My father is also here in Zürich and has hired a room in the St. Gotthard Hotel, Bahnhofstrasse, where we will have the party tomorrow."

"Now, let's forget everything for the time being and have some fun."

We arrived at his apartment and Sophie greeted me. The next day we took the Rolls Royce and drove to the hotel. His father greeted me and we walked to the private room. I thought it would be a big party, but to my surprise, I was the only guest apart from Paul's family. I had to smile; Dom Perignon and caviar as usual were available in abundance. It was a relaxed atmosphere and I was treated like one of the family.

After this, Paul drove us back to his apartment. I went to bed and my mind started working overtime again to digest the latest development.

The next morning Paul and I sat down and started talking.

CHAPTER 28

Could my life get weirder? It might.

*It is hard enough to remember my opinions, without also remembering my
reasons for them*

Friedrich Nietzsche

"Do you have to go back to Germany?" Paul asked.

"Not really; I have told the landlord that I will be away for
some time. Why, what have you got in mind?"

"I have started a business here in Zürich. I supply Dom
Perignon to some clubs and it is very profitable. Tonight we
are going to one of them and if you want you can help me"
he smiled.

"Look, if I join you I don't want to stay with you, as this
would not be fair to Sophie." I looked at him, "I want to do
something besides just helping you."

He bumped into someone by accident; a typical rocker, with an Elvis hairstyle and leather outfit. Didi looked at him and before he could apologise the guy went close to his face and said:

"What are you looking at me for? You got a problem?"

"What's your problem, mate?" he replied.

Without warning, the rocker punched him hard and the drinks went flying through the air. Didi retaliated by hitting him back. Then we saw the other members of the group leaving the bar and walking towards us. We knew we were in trouble. Didi jumped on the stage, where some cases with bottles were stored. Suddenly, Kubi and I were fighting some of the rockers back to back, whilst Didi tried to knock them out by throwing bottles at them. Finally, the bar staff broke the fight up and we left.

Festivals of all kinds sprang up everywhere during the summer months. Kubi invited me to go with all his friends to a '*Schützenfest*' *(a traditional shooting competition).*

It took place not far from where we lived. Ten of us went and settled on long wooden benches in a large tent. It was very busy. A brass band was playing traditional Swiss music and people were dancing. Kubi was the first to order a small carton of twelve miniature bottles of schnapps. More and more of these cartons appeared and someone decided to place them in the middle of the tent, starting to construct the Swiss cross. During the drinking session, Kubi said,

"Let's go and see who the best shot is".

We went to a stall, where we had to shoot with air rifles at some moving targets. By then we were already quite drunk. Kubi put his gun down to light a cigarette and, at the same time, he pulled the trigger by accident and shot himself in the foot. As he limped away, he got no sympathy from any of us, as we were rolling around in the grass with laughter. After more schnapps and singing, it was time to walk home. We set off well after midnight. None of us was able to walk in a straight line. Suddenly, Kubi took his shoes off and pushed them through the opening of a street gully.

"I never liked them," he mumbled and his expensive looking 'Al Capone' shoes disappeared. He carried on walking in his socks, as if nothing had changed.

I became tired and wanted to rest on a bench which I noticed on the other side of a fence. The metal fence was decorated with golden spikes. I decided to climb over it and got stuck on top. My weight slowly pushed the tips hard into my bottom as I tried to jump off. Unfortunately, the spikes went through my trousers, holding me firmly on the top of the fence. I ripped my trousers and finally, with bleeding buttocks, was able to jump down. My friends were nowhere to be seen. I was so drunk and tired that I fell asleep in somebody's front garden. In the morning a voice shouted:

"What the hell are you doing in my garden?" I got up, mumbled, "Sorry" and made my way home.

*

Paul was now living in Liechtenstein, where he had rented a nice house, and one day came to see me.

"Rudi, I need your help. I told you I am supplying clubs with champagne. It is not easy to park next to clubs and carry expensive cases of Dom Perignon into the premises so I need you to come with me to visit customers."

I was sure he really just wanted me as a companion.

"OK, as it happens, I've finished my DJ contract so I am free."

Next evening he picked me up and we drove to the popular Churchill nightclub at Bellevue, in the centre of Zürich. The manager greeted us and it became apparent that Paul was well known. He ordered a bottle of Dom Perignon and invited the bar staff to join us. The evening progressed and the club became very busy and noisy. The champagne started to have an effect, and I said to Paul,

"Bloody hell it's loud in here, it would be nice to have a bit of peace and quiet. You know the manager; tell him we want to talk to him, without all these people in here."

"Hey, John, I want to talk to you," he shouted. "We want to be alone for a while, get these people out of here"

"Are you crazy?" he replied, in disbelieve. "How on earth can I tell them to leave now? I would lose a lot of money."

"How much, for half an hour ?" Paul asked.

"At least four thousand Francs."

"OK, here is three thousand four hundred, put it in your pocket. Put the fire alarm on and let them back in, in half an hour. OK?"

Without waiting for John's answer, he put the amount on the bar. The fire alarm rang and all these well-groomed and expensively dressed guests had to leave. We had our own private club for some time, ordered another bottle and carried on chatting. Later, Paul laughed and said, "I suppose you'd better let them back in."

On our way out, Paul sold John two cases of champagne and with this; the evening was paid for partially.

My time as a disc jockey had now ended and become another part of my past life's rich tapestry. Now I was even more connected to Paul, both financially and mentally. The weirdness of my life continued and evolved, taking twists that were even more bizarre.

The principality of Liechtenstein was a magnet for many strange characters. As nobody had to declare their wealth, or pay taxes, it became a place of mystery, where nobody asked any financially related questions.

It was a strange place, filled with shiny Rolexes and expensive sunglasses. Groups of tourists would often relax in the expensive cafes, without realising the darker side of these beautiful mountainous surroundings.

Paul and Sophie fitted in like a glove. He now also rented an office with a small apartment attached. The property owner was an 'Honourable Ambassador' for the African Republic of Chad. I had my doubts that he had ever been in Chad or even knew where it was. Liechtenstein was THE place to buy aristocratic titles, residence permits for some dubious country, press passes or whatever somebody needed. You just had to name it.

I was now living between Zürich and Liechtenstein.

I stayed most of the time in Liechtenstein and life there was relaxing and for me problem free. I was always waiting to see what other rabbits Paul would pull out of the hat. I did not have to wait long. One morning we were sitting in glorious sunshine, on the terrace of our local café, in Vaduz, watching the world go by when I said,

"I am bored. Let's drive somewhere, just to see some life."

"What do you suggest?" Paul asked.

"Well, you remember in Hamburg when we just packed our bags and drove to Sweden?"

"Yes?" He looked at me with enthusiasm.

"I want to go somewhere to have a nice piece of cake, maybe the famous 'Sacher Torte'."

"Let me check something out," he smiled. A few minutes later, he came back and sat down. "I tell you what. You said you want a Sacher Torte. OK. I've just found out there is a flight leaving Zürich for Vienna in three hours. Let's take that plane and then a taxi to the Sacher Hotel and have a piece of cake."

We jumped in the Rolls Royce, drove to the Kloten airport, and flew first class to Vienna. We then took a taxi to the Sacher Hotel, ate our piece of cake and flew back.

After this, I drove back to Zürich for a few weeks. On one weekend I went with friends to their chalet high up in the Alps and had some memorable days in the fresh air with views to die for.

Ten days later Paul got in touch with me again. " Can we meet at the Baur au Lac hotel at four this afternoon?"

"What is the rush? Anything happened?"

"No, no. I just want to talk to you, OK?"

We met in the hotel and had a coffee. "Listen, do you fancy a trip to the South of France?"

I shrugged my shoulders, which confirmed I was up for it.

"OK, let's go. I will drive you home to get your things and then you can stay with us tonight in Liechtenstein."

We walked down to the hotel garage. I was looking for the Rolls Royce. Instead he walked up to a brand new Porsche

911. I did not blink an eyelid or say anything, as we had been here before. Next morning we jumped in the car and drove towards the South of France. Just outside Montpellier we noticed a dark, smelly bloom of smoke and with a massive bang the engine blew up. Paul got on the phone to Porsche in Germany and after a long debate they agreed to fly out a new engine and paid for our hotel.

In 1970, just one and a half years after the Russian invasion, we decided to drive to Prague. The Prague Spring reforms of 1968 were an attempt by President Dubcek to grant additional rights to the citizens of Czechoslovakia. The country was full of hope and freedom, but the government was quickly toppled by the Russian occupiers and the President was arrested.

We arrived at our hotel near Wenceslas Square. The receptionist advised us to park the car somewhere safe, as they could not provide a secured garage on site. Consequently, wherever we parked, we had some police protecting the Porsche, as inevitably crowds would surround the car, to get a glance of it.

Czechoslovakia was still in the grip of Russia. There were restrictions on food and other commodities. We spoke to some young people who particularly suffered, with lack of education and no access to universities. If their family was on the wrong side of the political scale, they had a problem. Even travel was restricted, as they were allowed only to visit countries within the Eastern Block. Just to survive was a daily struggle for many people, as there was a shortage of all essential commodities, like bread, meat and most of all fruit and veg.

We spoke to many people, and got an insight into their suffering. For Paul and me it was exactly the opposite, as everything was unimaginably cheap.

After our stay in Prague, we carried on to Budapest, which had also suffered greatly after the 1956 Russian invasion, when over six thousand Hungarians had died in the struggle to defend their country. When we visited, the country was still under the iron fist of Russia. However, the city had a feel of elegance and openness. We dined in traditional restaurants where small gipsy bands played the most beautiful music.

We left Hungary after four days, and returned to Liechtenstein.

CHAPTER 29

A journey into my past

Sometimes the questions are complicated and the answers are simple

Dr. Seuss

It was a warm, sunny Saturday in Zürich and I was getting ready to meet my friends in a restaurant. We planned to have lunch and then make our way to the river Limmat. Most sunny days we met and relaxed on a decking at the riverbank from which we dived into the river. I was just on the way out of my apartment, when I received a call from my sister in Germany,

"Rudi?" When I heard her voice, I knew something was not right. "Our father is in hospital. He is seriously ill. He has cancer and the doctors told me, he has only a week or so to live."

I totally stiffened, as my darkest time now caught up with me. A sudden flashback took my breath away. I was numb and my legs felt like jelly.

"Are you still there?"

"Yes."

"He wants to see you. Can you come to Hamburg, he is in the hospital?"

"Renate, I am in Zürich," was the only thing I could reply.

"Please, come to see him. It would mean a lot to him. He wants to make peace with you. Please bear in mind, he is dying."

I could hear her crying. I had to sit down for my brain was somersaulting. I felt dizzy. It was like a bad dream, as my past memories with him returned. A fight started raging within me and many questions appeared which needed answers. Can I forget what he has done to me? Can I forget how he destroyed our family, how he humiliated and punished me? Has he ever enquired how I was, where I was, or what had become of me? The answer to all of these was no. However, in the end, my answer was simple. If I refused to see and talk to him, would I be any different from him?

"Renate, I will book a flight for tomorrow and go straight from the airport to him. I will fly back the same day."

"Thank you," she replied, with a tear drenched voice. "Can you not stay for the funeral?"

I did not reply and let her find her own interpretation and we said goodbye.

Next morning, I went to Kloten to catch the flight to Hamburg. I took a taxi to the hospital and after locating the ward, I opened the door to his room. The same smell and atmosphere hit me. This familiar feeling of death, as I had experienced with my mother, overwhelmed me. Only the circumstances and my emotions on this visit were miles apart. There he was old and grey, like a bundle of misery. All the strength in him I once feared was gone. I felt some sadness, as I walked through the door. Then he saw me; his eyes widened as he tried to sit up.

"Rudi," escaped his thin lips.

"Renate told me that you are ill and asked me to come and see you," I replied.

"Yes, I am dying; I have incurable cancer and not long to live," he said in weak voice. Then he started crying: "Son, I don't want to die. I am frightened."

I stood there next to his bed and said nothing.

"Please put this pillow behind my back, I want to talk to you."

I made him comfortable so that he was able to sit up.

"I know I was not the best father and have let you down. Can you forgive me?"

I could not answer, as his question astounded me. What should I say? I was searching within myself for a solution.

In the end I just looked at him and said, "Yes, it's OK", in a gentle voice.

He stretched his hand out, which I took. He pulled me towards him, which I let him do. Then he attempted to kiss me. I stood firm and instead shook his hand. I looked at him and now I felt pity. There was nothing in me that I could have given him. Still, I held his hand, as his tears ran down his grey haggard face. Were these tears of regret or of self-pity, in coming to terms with the inevitable? I leaned over him and looked into his eyes for the last time.

"I have to go. I want to see grandma." I nearly said,' the one you kicked out of our home, but I bit my tongue. " I have to go back to Switzerland," I said instead.

"Please stay a while," he implored, but I shook my head, said good-bye, and left the room.

Outside, the whole event went through my head. Should I have reacted differently? Should I have hugged him and let him kiss me? I realised I could not have done it. I had done my bit to make peace and hoped that it might have lightened his burden.

I was now on my way to see my grandma for the last time in my life. After our family breakup, she had found refuge and peace in a catholic nursing home. In the calm atmosphere of her little room, we looked at each other, but for a while were not able to talk. Like an unspoken understanding, neither of us wanted to reminisce over the tragedy of our past and tears filled our eyes. I took her in my arms and held her. My tears started to flow uncontrollably. I held her tight, to protect her, as she had held me in her arms so often. This beautiful woman, my bastion and guardian, looked at me and whispered the words I will not forget

"Rudi, may God protect you," and as she had done so many times in my childhood, marked my forehead with the sign of the cross. "I am tired," was her way of saying good-bye.

I took her face in my hands and gave her a final kiss. I got up and looked at her and as I went to the door, I turned around and for the last time took her vision with me to cherish. An emotional farewell without words, but replaced by mutual understanding. I closed her door. Two weeks later, she passed away.

Oma was an extra ordinary, strong woman. She lost her husband in the First World War as a very young mother of three children, later lost her two sons in the Second World War. Between all these tragedies, she found the strength to adopt a child. She had to flee from her home in unimaginable circumstances, to save her family from falling into the hands of Russian soldiers. Finally, after finding safety and security in Hamburg, she saw her daughter die of a terrible illness.

I will never forget her.

CHAPTER 30

Africa here I come, are you ready for me?

Life is either a daring adventure or nothing at all

Helen Keller

My life took another unexpected, consequential and wide reaching turn.

The Principality of Liechtenstein was celebrating the sixty-fifth birthday of the ruling Prince. During the festivities in Vaduz, tables and long wooden benches were set out and restaurants and temporary bars sold everything to lighten the public's mood. It was a beautiful sunny, summer's day, morphing into a warm, pleasant evening. I was sitting with friends chatting, and drinking, when suddenly, somebody tapped me on the shoulder.

"Are you German?" the person asked.

I turned around, "Yes."

"What are all these festivities about?" he asked me in German.

I explained to him that today was a public holiday, to celebrate the birthday of the Big Boss in the castle and that was the reason why so many people were enjoying themselves.

"Are you living in Vaduz?" he asked.

"From time to time, as my friend has an office here. Come on, sit down and have a drink, "I replied.

He introduced himself as Hans and said he was here on holiday. We started to chat.

"I am originally from Augsburg, South Germany, but have been living for many years in Kenya, on the coast, in Mombasa. I left Germany to avoid the compulsory Military Service."

He sat down and we started drinking. The wine and beer was flowing, and I realised that I was quite drunk.

He asked me about the business I was involved in and after my explanation, said,

"You should come to Mombasa; there are great possibilities to make good money. I am flying back tomorrow. Why don't you come with me and have a good look around. If you like it, you could maybe consider doing business there, and if it is not your cup of tea, at least you can see something of Kenya."

I heard one of my drunken voices shouting, 'Heh, slow down you don't know this guy.' The other, 'why not, what have you got to lose, the worst that can happen is a nice holiday?'

"I'll come with you, let's go," I said, before my brain could analyse this statement. "Hans", I mumbled, "I'll book the flight tomorrow morning. Now let's celebrate our friendship."

Next morning I packed a couple of things in a small suitcase. I called Paul and told him I was on my way to Kenya. I heard him laughing down the phone.

"Are you completely crazy? What do you want to do there?" he asked in a disbelieving voice.

"I will be in touch," I said and hung up.

I met Hans at his hotel and we flew in the afternoon to Mombasa. Only when we were mid-air did it dawn on me, what I had done. Actually, I didn't even know who Hans was, what he did, where I was going, where I would stay or what to expect. I had no knowledge of Kenya, let alone Mombasa. During the fight, Hans explained to me, that he was a manager of an optician's shop in Mombasa and was married to a woman from the Seychelles. All this sounded very exotic and exciting. Maybe I was ready for a change, ready for some adventure.

After fourteen hours, we landed in Kenya. It was in the spring of 1973 when I set foot for the first time in Africa, a continent that I embraced instantly. The minute I stepped out of the airport building, I sensed exotic smells that filled my nostrils, a mixture of spices, indigenous timber, like mahogany, yellow wood and fever tree. It is difficult for me to describe the hustle and bustle that is so unique to Africa. Within seconds, and without any knowledge or reason, I loved this place! We went through customs and walked out into the warm African evening. I was enchanted by and totally immersed into its atmosphere. I absorbed whatever was on display. The colourfully dressed women, shouting and the hustle and energy of the locals astounded me. I had stepped into a different world.

We took a taxi into town and arrived in the centre of Mombasa. Hans asked the driver to stop in the Kilindini Road, the main street.

"I'll let you out here. There is the Hotel Splendid, book yourself in and I will call you." With this he drove off.

Now, I stood on my own, with no idea where I was. I made my way to the hotel. Thank God, I had some dollars on me, and booked myself a room. It became very quickly apparent, that this place 'Splendid' was well known for special female entertainment, as the women standing in and around the hotel confirmed. I collapsed onto the not so clean bed, as my long travels caught up with me. My head was spinning, ' What had I let myself into?' Just before I switched the light off, I noticed a couple of small lizards, one above me on the ceiling, and his mate staring at me from the opposite wall. They freaked me out, but I learnt later that these fellows were geckos, and thankfully took care of mosquitos and other nasty insects.

Next morning, I stepped out of the hotel, into glorious sunshine. I stood, overwhelmed, trying to take in the most colourful picture of organised chaos taking place in front of me. Cars, motor scooters and bikes were fighting each other, to make the first move, because it seemed everybody was in a hurry. Women with baskets on their beautifully decorated heads, with babies strapped to their backs, walked through the traffic, without a second thought. The noise was overwhelming, but I absorbed it as exotic music. I just could not move away from this scene. I wanted to take it all in.

My eyes focussed on a young man on a bicycle, who had his head held high, expressing an attitude of 'not having a care in the world'. His lips were moving, giving the impression he was singing. Live chickens were hanging secured on the handlebar on each side of his bike. Just in front of him, stood an older man leaning, on a broomstick, having a rest from sweeping the road. I watched this unfolding drama with great anticipation, as the biker got closer to the old man, without noticing him. Suddenly, he drove over the broomstick on which the man was leaning. The broom flew in the air and the old road sweeper collapsed onto the road. The young man flew over the handlebars and landed in a heap on top of him. Some of the chickens seized this opportunity to fly away. The pair of them got up, and an almighty argument started between them, watched by a laughing crowd. This mayhem carried on for some time, until they both dusted themselves down and left the scene.

The spectators moved on, as if such an incident was common occurrence. I stood there, smiling, thinking, what would the reaction in Europe have been? I realised more and more, I have stepped into a different world.

WELCOME TO MOMBASA – TO KENYA – TO AFRICA

CHAPTER 31

Welcome to Africa!

Be the change that you wish to see in the world

Mahatma Gandhi

I waited for another hour to see if Hans was coming to meet me, then I walked down the Kilindini Road, which housed a monumental landmark of two huge elephant tusks, forming an arc that dwarfed the road. I ended up at a restaurant called The Manor House. As it happened, its terrace was the hangout of many expats. I ordered a beer and started talking to some of them. There was a mixture of locals, Brits, Germans and Swiss, enjoying a relaxing drinking atmosphere. I introduced myself and we exchanged information. From this, I gained a good idea why so many came to work or settle in Mombasa.

"By the way, I am Urs. Meet Steve, he is originally from the UK, and Werner from Germany. Steve owns a coffee plantation in Tanzania, and Werner is the manager of a hotel in Nyali."

We shook hands and they invited me for another beer.

"Are you a tourist here?" Urs asked

"To be honest, I have no idea whether I will stay and start a business or have a holiday and go back," was my reply. "I currently live in Zürich and recently met someone there who lives here. He encouraged me to come and have a look, to see if I like it."

He smiled, "I am from Basle. I was fed up with all the bureaucracy in Switzerland, and looked for a change. That's why I'm here."

"What are you doing here now; I mean what business are you in?" I asked.

"Well, I took all my savings and bought a second hand Land Rover and now take tourists on safari, here in Kenya as well as in Tanzania."

"Sounds very interesting, would you have any advice for me? I am open to all suggestions, as I have no fixed plan or idea what to do. By the way, I just arrived last night."

"I think you might enjoy it here," Werner said. "There are plenty of opportunities, if you know your way around, and have the right connections," he smiled. "Listen, if you are serious and want to start a business here, let us know. We are happy to help, the clocks are ticking differently here, than in Europe, so you will need the right contacts to succeed. Are you from Hamburg? I think I noticed your accent."

"Yes, I was born in Lübeck, but grew up in Hamburg. I live now between Zürich and Liechtenstein," I explained.

"I'm from Hamburg Bergedorf. It's always nice to know somebody from the same place, when you are in a completely different country," Werner replied. After this chat, we established a special relationship.

"Thanks. I think the first thing I have to get used to the heat and humidity. I already sweat like a pig. There is only one way to overcome this problem, let's have another beer." With this gesture, I made three good and helpful friends. We had some more beer and suddenly Hans appeared and joined us. It was a promising start.

I said good-bye to my new friends and we went to Hans's optician shop. He was the only optician in Mombasa. He taught me a lot about living here and how to start a new business. We discussed various possibilities and opportunities.

"Look, for instance, safaris are very popular. However, many people like Urs, whom you just met, are already doing it. Whatever business you decide to get into, first, you need a local partner, who has to own fifty-one percent of your business. Without that, you would not get a trade licence to form your company. You will also need a residence permit to stay in Kenya. You have to obtain it from the government in Nairobi, which might not be easy. You will also need a bank account here to pay all the government's fees and conduct your financial business. Let's have a break and a beer."

I realised that his speech was slightly slurry and his eyes looked glazed. Later, I found out that he had been taking some substances. On a number of occasions, this would be obvious, even on some of our business trips.

"What about dealing in gemstones?" He suggested. "I could introduce you to a friend of mine; he owns a jewellery shop that sells Tanzanite, Sapphire and some beautiful yellow and green Tzavonite. If you consider this as a business, you could sell to the tourists."

During our visit to the jewellery shop, I received further detailed information, and made up my mind. I wanted to be in the gemstone business. Hans also introduced me to a well-known gemstone cutter, named Ashura. He agreed to work for me and gave me a list of the machinery, tools and essential materials he would need to create a finished gemstone. I decided to fly back to Switzerland to buy what was needed.

"Ashura, I will employ you when I'm back." I told him confidently.

I flew back to Zürich and bought all the items he required. I spent some days with my friends but avoided contact with Paul, as I did not want to listen to any more of his reasons for me to stay.

On my return to the airport in Mombasa, I went through customs and had to explain to the duty officer what I needed all my items for. During the interrogation, I also mentioned that I was in the process of forming a company and was now looking for a local business partner. Suddenly he seemed very interested and his attitude changed completely. After a further fifteen minutes talk, I had a new partner. His first contribution was to let me through customs without any further questions or duty payment.

Later we met in town, making our partnership official with some bottles of beer and agreed on our trade name: MZURI GEMSTONE LLC. Michael Karimi, the customs officer, became a good friend and a big asset. The main reason I had selected him was that he knew how to import items very easily, and had access to local authorities, as his brother was in a high position in the government.

I met my new friends on a regular basis, as the Manor House terrace was the centre of gossip. On such a day, Urs said to me,

"You told us you had never been to Africa before. Would you like to come with me on safari in Tsavo National Park? This might give you an idea about what Kenya has to offer. I will pick you up tomorrow morning."

"Wow, thanks. I'd appreciate that."

Internally, I screamed with delight, anticipation, and thought Christmas and my birthday had fallen on the same day. Next morning I jumped in his Land Rover and we drove to the Tzavo National Park. The rangers greeted us at the entrance to the safari park. We bypassed some tourist groups and went straight in, without any payment. It appeared they knew Urs well.

We did not have to wait too long before zebras, wildebeest and gazelles crossed our path. It seemed, as if Urs had arranged for the animals to parade in front of us. My camera worked at top speed. I photographed just about everything that moved. It was just breath- taking, seeing all the colours, and hearing the different noises. For me, the whole landscape looked, as if I had just stepped into paradise. Then a huge elephant suddenly appeared out of the bush. Noticing us, he stopped and his ears stood up. Urs switched the engine off. We were only ten metres apart, the silence gave this beautiful giant confidence, and with his trunk, he started ripping some branches off a tree. I was mesmerised and overwhelmed by this fascinating spectacle.

MY FIRST WILD ELEPHANT.

Over excitedly I pointed my camera towards this impressive animal. It was a dream come true. I nearly stopped breathing, 'Click'… I had no film left.

"God damn shit!" Was all I could shout and I threw the camera into the back of the car.

My location had changed, but not my temper. I was still a small-minded idiot. Maybe there was hope for me here, to change my attitude, as the pace of life was much slower and things, that were important in Europe, are of no great consequence here in Africa.

Urs nearly killed himself laughing: "Don't worry you'll have plenty of other opportunities" he said, with tears rolling down his cheeks. After a while, the elephant moved on and we continued our safari.

During this time of year, everything was green and lush, a complete picture postcard. I never took a camera on any trip or safari again and therefore, to this day, have no evidence that I ever saw a wild animal.

Slowly, I started to take my surroundings in, as my brain advised me, and I began to open my eyes and to realise how fortunate I was to be able to explore Kenya, Africa, and hopefully the world. It was a first step in experiencing a different, maybe more useful education, which I had missed in my school years. What I had learned on this beautiful trip was *'Insight is the first step in the right direction.''* Travel became one of the greatest driving forces in my life.

At the end of the trip, we had a drink during our stop in Void, a small town at the edge of the park. I felt, I had experienced something beautiful, although I had nothing to show for it.

"Urs, you wouldn't know by any chance where I could rent an apartment in Mombasa? I have decided to stay here and start a gemstone business," I announced.

"Congratulations! I am very happy for you and glad you want to stay." He shook my hand.

I rented an apartment in a block of four in the district of Nyali, half a mile in the bush, via a small sandy way, a stone's throw away from a small local settlement. Coconut trees surrounded my new home. It had a communal swimming pool and a spectacular view over the countryside towards the Indian Ocean. I thought I was in the Garden of Eden, very different from my upbringing in the council house in Hamburg.

*

Horst and I had agreed before I left Germany that he owed me around ten thousand Mark, because of the failed property deal in Lanzarote. I got in touch with him and he came to visit me in Mombasa. He had organised a shipment of a Mercedes Benz car to Mombasa and gave me a set of keys. Some weeks later, the shipping company informed me, the car was at the port. As I had a key, I just walked straight into the free port and drove it away, thus avoiding the very high import duties. I parked the car in front of my apartment, asked our security guard to clean it, and went for a nap.

"What the hell are you doing?" I shouted when I came back.

"You asked me to clean the car," he replied.

"Are you really that stupid?"

He was sitting in the car with a hosepipe, spraying the inside of the car. The seats were soaking wet, with the glove compartment dripping with water. I was not quite sure if I should laugh or cry.

In the afternoon, after the car had dried out, I met Werner and Steve at the Manor House and parked the car in front of it. We were sitting on the terrace, having a beer, when two police officers approached me.

"Is this your car?" they asked, pointing at the Mercedes.

"Yes," I replied "Why? What is the problem?" I asked sheepishly.

"You were observed driving the car out of the free port, avoiding paying the import duty."

"Are you arresting me?" It was the second time I had asked this question in my lifetime.

"No, but you have to come with us to the police station, we need you to answer questions."

There was no doubt that he would not take no for an answer. My friends got worried and asked if there was anything, they could do to help.

"No," I replied, I will let you know later what is going on."

The two officers got in the car with me, and we drove to the police station. There, the officer repeated the charge.

"Somebody saw you, driving the car out of the free port, without paying any import duty. This could be very serious."

The way he said '*could*,' indicated to me that there might be some room for negotiation, as I remembered from previous experiences. Realising I could be in deep trouble, I asked him,

"Please, could you call my partner, he is a customs officer, and might help clarify what went wrong."

He nodded his head and then asked his partner to leave the room. My business partner, Michael Karimi came in and started speaking to the officer in Swahili. After half an hour, Michael turned to me.

"Could you do something for him?"

"What does he want, cash or some gemstones? Please ask him what he prefers." He translated my suggestions to the officer.

"He would like some watches," Michael explained

"OK. I will bring some watches back from my next trip to Switzerland, for him and his family." Again, Michael conversed in Swahili and then shook hands with the smiling officer. An agreement had been reached, and a few weeks later, I met the officer and gave him the promised watches. I even took him for a beer.

We shook hands and he said, "Thank you, my wife will be very happy. Should you ever need any help, just come and see me."

I stayed in touch with him. Another insurance policy was always useful.

I met my friends and explained what had happened. They seemed not too surprised.

"This type of 'oiling the wheels ' is normal," Steve said. "Urs has told you that I run a coffee plantation in Tanzania. You will not believe what I have to do to stay in business. Most months I get visitors, from either the government or soldiers. They demand money and remind me that I am a muzungu (foreigner), and that they can kick me out anytime they choose. Tell this to somebody in Europe, and they will understand what racism is," he said shaking his head, "It does not make any difference that I have been here for over ten years as a resident in the country." He lit another cigarette. "I come to Mombasa to relax and get away from the pressure for a while. Whenever you are in Tanzania, come and see me, but I warn you, my plantation is miles away from any civilisation and not easy to find," he smiled. He handed me a piece of paper with all the details of how to get there.

"Thanks, I appreciate that," I replied gratefully.

Then Werner gave me another example of something that had happened here in Mombasa.

"A foreign delegation came on an official visit to Kenya and presented the Government with six new Mercedes Benz cars for its Diplomatic Corps. As soon as they had left, these brand new cars started life as a private taxi business. This, of course, had an impact on some people in Mombasa. It seemed, some influential members of the government had an interest in this business and they announced that any old taxis were no longer allowed to collect passengers from the airport. Officially, the government had decided that old taxis were not a good image for the country of Kenya. Therefore, all old cars were banned and the drivers lost their jobs."

I must admit, I was surprised that some of these old taxis were still in service. One of the drivers I used quite frequently had no ignition key anymore, and the engine only started by short-circuiting the ignition cables.

*

My friend Werner gave me this advice. "Rudi if you need anything in future that requires some help, go to Khimji, he is the mafia boss here. He knows everything and everybody but make sure you don't rub him up the wrong way, he could become nasty"

Now I had most things in place to start my business, only my trade licence was missing. I drove to Nairobi and spoke to a clerk about the necessary paperwork.

"You have to fill in the forms first. It will take at least two weeks before we can issue the permit."

After two weeks, I went back. "No, not ready, come back next week," was his short explanation. I was furious.

After my third trip on the treacherous Mombasa to Nairobi road, I smelt a rat; I went to the bank and withdrew some money. I returned to the clerk's office and banged the briefcase on his table, unlocked it and turned it towards him. I had my licence within five minutes. With some extra shillings, I also got a separate licence for dealing in Tanzanite.

I had to drive back to Mombasa in the dark. I was sure no European insurance company would have covered me for such a trip. I learned very quickly, during my trips to and from Nairobi that the best time to travel by road is at the beginning of the month, because police controlling the roads have just received their salary. During any other time it was not so easy to avoid paying bribes. Only once, I argued not to pay and held for two hours, whilst they inspected my car very slowly. After this, I always kept a jar of coins in my car. Sometimes these control posts were only five hundred metres apart, and I did not bother to close my window, as I simply handed out coins, between the stops. The funny thing was that no words were exchanged during such transactions.

The highway between Nairobi and Mombasa was like dicing with death. Half way home, I had to hit my brakes hard; as a rhino crossed the road in front of me (I had no camera to prove it). Road signs indicating the crossing of elephants should have warned me that something like this could happen at any time. I had to smile when I compared the elephant sign to the ones in Europe, of ducks and cows. On this seven-hour drive, I had God knows how many near misses, avoiding lorries without headlights, that were driving on the wrong side, or overtaking on corners, and animals trying to discover if the grass was greener on the other side of the road.

Next day I met Khimji, the underworld king and fixer of Mombasa. I introduced myself and we shook hands. He was of Indian origin, as small as he was wide, with dark darting eyes. We discussed living here in general and then I asked him about the gemstone business.

"Rudi, you will have to be very careful, there will be plenty of crooks trying to rob or cheat you."

This advice came from the mouth of, apparently, the biggest crook in Mombasa.

"If you organise your business well and concentrate on the tourists, you might be OK."

"I already have a licence and employ a recommended cutter and polisher," I mentioned.

He smiled. "Wow, you do work fast."

I thought his voice contained a tone of admiration. We said good-bye and his parting words were, "If you need any help, you know where to find me."

"You never know," I thought to myself, "I might just need his help one day."

CHAPTER 32

Ready for business

Don't be pushed around by the fears in your mind. Be led by the dreams in your heart

Roy T. Bennett

Ashura spread the word that we were in the business of buying raw, uncut gemstones. At the beginning, there were many crooks and imposters, trying to cheat us, suppliers of all kinds of stones approached us. Ashura scrupulously examined every item offered and they soon realised that they could not screw us over. We bought some samples of gemstones, just to test the prices and grades, and then selected the reliable and trustworthy suppliers. We started working from my apartment, but I conducted all business meetings at the Manor House hotel.

One day a couple of new dealers came to speak to me.

"We have a large amount of Tanzanite for sale, if you are interested."

"Yes, I might be. Let me have a look."

They explained that the owner of these stones lived in Tanzania, was a local man and would not travel outside his area. The only thing they could suggest was that, I should go to Tanzania to negotiate with him directly. They said it was an interesting lot and the value of the stones was around forty thousand Kenyan Shillings.

"OK", I said, "tell your friend that we are willing to come and see him. Give me the details of the place where we can meet and I'll let you know if and when we can come to meet."

Off they went, and I thought, this could be an opportunity to start dealing in these expensive Tanzanite stones. The next day I met with Urs.

"Urs, would you come with me to Tanzania, as I want to meet a local man there to buy gemstones? Of course I will pay you".

"Yes, my safari business is quiet at the moment, and I'm happy to come with you."

"Thanks, I'll let you know when and where we are going".

I discussed the whole issue with Ashura and Michael. Ashura said, "It is a bit unusual for these men to come to see you, trying to sell you stones, without showing you any samples or giving you more details. Let me make some enquiries and see if we can get more information about these guys."

Three days later, we met at the hotel. He had some bad news for me.

"I heard that they are crooks. You remember they mentioned an amount of forty thousand. My contact told me, they have done this before. They want to meet you in a secluded place and rob you."

"Wow!" was all I could say. After some consideration, I said, "I think we have to teach those guys a lesson. I am new here and if I do not stop this sort of thing in its tracks, we might not be taken seriously in the future. Ashura, contact these bastards and tell them we will be at their chosen place next Friday afternoon. Leave the rest to me."

I went to meet Werner at his hotel and explained my situation.

"Werner, Urs told me that you are running the air rifle club. Would it be possible to borrow a couple of rifles and one pistol? I do not need any live ammunition. I just need to show some crooks they can't mess with me,"

He looked at me and started laughing. "No problem, welcome to Kenya. You just have to promise me, if the guns are lost or damaged, you will pay for them."

"OK, not a problem. The other thing I want to ask you is, would it be possible to put one glass display case with my cut stones in your hotel shop? I will pay you a commission on each sale?"

"Sounds good to me, I will talk to other hotel managers I know and you can maybe do the same in their hotels. Rudi, I know you live now in Nyali, if you ever want to come and have lunch or dinner in the hotel, feel free. Just mention my name."

"Thanks, Werner you have helped me a lot. I am starting to feel at home here, although it seems I have to overcome some hurdles."

I smiled and put the two rifles, the pistol and some blank cartridges in my car and went to see Ashura. "Are you OK to come with me to Tanzania to see these fake dealers?"

"No problem, we'll meet them near Muhezu, it's a small settlement," he replied.

I then went to meet Urs to explain the situation. He was also up for it. On Friday morning, we drove from Mombasa, crossing the border into Tanzania towards Tanga. Ashura had no passport but crossing the border was no problem, as some Kenya Shillings are as good as your passport.

We stopped just outside a local village surrounded by bushland. I asked Ashura and Urs to lie down in the car with the two guns. We were waiting. Suddenly the same two guys who came to see me in Mombasa stepped out of the bush. One of them had a gun in his hand. I let them come nearer and when they were ten yards from our Land Rover, I opened the door, pointed my pistol and gave a warning shot. Urs and Ashura, jumped out of the car brandishing their rifles.

Ashura shouted at the gunman in Swahili, "Drop that thing, otherwise we will shoot."

He dropped the gun as if it were a hot piece of steel and put his hands up in the air. I had no idea what 'Don't fuck with us,' is in Swahili, but they must have got the message. I went up to them.

"Listen, you chose the wrong people here. If you are serious and want to do business with us, I am telling you and your friends, to come to Mombasa. I will forget this little episode and we can do some business in the future, but now get the hell out of here! By the way, I will keep your gun as a souvenir and payment for our expenses."

As soon as they were gone, I sat down and said, "Bloody hell, I nearly wet myself when they came towards us with that gun."

On the way back, we stopped near the border and had a meal and plenty to drink. "I think we showed these lowlife punks that we are no pushover. I hope they will pass the message on." I said.

The word must have spread. From that moment on, I became a member of the community and respected as a business person of some standing. I changed from a muzungu (foreigner) to a rafiki (friend). Locals started to greet me and I felt great.

I hired Urs to accompany me on other trips to buy stones directly from villagers in Kenya and Tanzania. We stopped in small villages, in the middle of nowhere. I would sit in the Land Rover, while queues of local folks lined up in front of me. I inspected the stones they offered and then haggled the price. I bought these raw stones, which Ashura then transformed into beautiful sellable merchandise. It was certainly not your normal business procedure.

I settled in to my new surroundings, my paradise, quite easily. The apartment was both my office and a beautiful home, cleaned once a week by a young local. I only had to step out of my veranda door and I could then jump into the pool. The young gardener was very happy, to climb up the palm trees and throw coconuts into the pool for me. Then he would cut one open and I had the freshest coconut milk, which I often mixed with Bacardi. Near the pool was a communal bar, where we sometimes held parties. In the mornings after, I often saw monkeys moving in a peculiar way. I realised they had finished off drinking the bottles of beer we had left the night before. They were drunk.

*

One evening, I was sitting on the terrace of the Manor House hotel and met Thomas, who was also from Germany.

"What are you doing here in Mombasa?" I asked. After a drink or two, he told me, that he was in trouble with the Kenyan police.

"I was involved in an accident. A friend of mine was driving, drunk, uninsured and hit another car. He was injured, nothing too serious, but still needed hospital treatment," he lit a cigarette, with shaking hands. "I know it was wrong, but my mate told me, just vanish, otherwise they will arrest both of us. I was also drunk and panicked and ran away. The police are still looking for me."

This had apparently happened in Nairobi where he lived.

"I had to get the hell out of Nairobi and I knew somebody here, but unfortunately he has moved."

"So, where will you stay? Are you saying the police are looking for you here as well?"

"I really don't know, but I can't take the risk. I even feel uncomfortable sitting here, just in case. You never know. I am shit scared."

"Thomas, let me help you. You can stay in my apartment, until you are safe to go back to Nairobi or Germany."

"Rudi, I have no money, I left everything behind."

"It's OK, you don't have to pay me. So don't worry."

"I promise, I will pay you back when I am able to return to Nairobi, thanks."

He moved in with me, and did not leave the apartment at all.

A week later, Paul called me. "Rudi, you have to come to Liechtenstein, I need to talk to you. Your flight is booked for next Monday. I will pick you up from the airport in Zürich. See you then."

I wondered why he needed to see me so urgently, something drastic must have happened. The flight was in the evening.

"Thomas, I need to be at the airport around eight o'clock. I will take my car to the airport. Will you come with me so you can return it to Mombasa and put it into a go-down garage until I am back? If you have any problems, go to Khimji and mention my name, he will help you."

I think, with hindsight that that must have been one of my biggest mistakes, as I was to discover later. It made me think more carefully before trusting people, I did not know well.

After a delayed flight of over twenty hours, Paul picked me up. "Let's drive to Vaduz and I will explain it all to you," he was as mysterious as ever. We arrived at his house, sat down and I listened.

Paul looked very serious.

"I needed to tell you in person what is happening as it's going to change everything. I have had some people from the council, visiting us. They pointed out that we are now living illegally in Liechtenstein, as our residence permits have expired. They have given us one-month's grace time. After that, we have to leave Liechtenstein, or we'll be deported back to Germany."

He paused. For the first time ever, I saw him look very worried and nervous.

"There is no way, I can go back to Germany, and I think that there might also be arrest warrants out for me in some other European countries. Therefore, I can't take any chance or risk and must settle somewhere other than in Europe."

We looked at each other and in his eyes; I could see the mirrored consequences of his past actions. I asked myself, is Paul's future starting to slip away from him and his family? Is the person, who always found a way out of the tightest spot, now, facing an unassailable obstacle?

No, this story had another twist!

"You remember the owner I rented our office in Liechtenstein from? He is an 'Honourable Ambassador' for the African Republic of Chad," he smiled. "You always said you had your doubts that he had ever been in Chad or even knew where it was. I spoke to him and asked him if he could help. He is going to arrange a passport for me."

I swallowed hard. I just could not believe what I was hearing. "Seriously, how the hell will anybody take you as a Chad citizen?"

"Let me worry about that", was his answer. "He arranged a meeting with some Ministers in Chad and I am flying out next week."

I was speechless.

"I get all the paperwork, citizenship, residence address and passport. He will also organise a government document that shows I am a political activist threatened with a jail term. Therefore, I have to leave my country of residence. You follow me?"

"No," I replied startled. "You have been through a lot of shit, but this takes the biscuit. It must cost a fortune?"

"Whatever it costs, it has to be done. The starting price is fifty thousand US dollars. However, I am sure the contacts in Chad will try to milk it more. We will see. He also has some contacts in Canada and I will apply for refugee status over there. I intend to live permanently in Canada."

"You will do what?" I shouted and shook my head in disbelief.

"Yep, you heard it here first," he smiled," in the meantime, Sophie will stay with some friends in Germany and she will join me in Canada when I have settled and all is safe. Let us have some fun days here, before you go back to Kenya. Funny, who would have thought, that we would both make business in Africa."

We tried to laugh, but it did not work. Sophie joined us, and the three of us went out for dinner. Somehow, we had a pleasant evening, and forgot for a moment what the future had in store.

The next day, on the way back to the airport, he said, "I'll be in touch with you, as soon as I settle in Canada and find the right place to live."

At the airport in Kloten, we shook hands. I looked at him, "Listen, you know I'll be there if you need me."

He looked very emotional: "Thanks, for saying that," was all he could mumble.

We went our separate ways, but both of us knew somehow that we would meet again. I never knew another person that lived in such a fast lane of life. Later, he informed me that a few days after our meeting, he had flown to Chad and from there went directly to Vancouver and applied for refugee status.

I returned to Mombasa and tried to contact Thomas from the airport, but without success. I took a taxi home and realised immediately he was gone. The next day I went into town and walked into Khimji's shop. Since my gemstones dealing, we had had several meetings.

"Khimji, I have a problem. I gave shelter to a German. He is in his mid-twenties, blond and tall. Did he contact you?" Khimji looked at me a bit sheepishly.

"Sit down, yes; he came to see me three days ago. He was in a very agitated mood and very nervous, and he looked over his shoulder every five minutes. He asked me, if I could help him to get out of the country, preferably to Tanzania, and said he would pay. I asked him why, what is the urgency? He told me, that he had killed a girl in a road accident here in Mombasa and done a runner. "

In that moment I realised, what a stupid mistake I made, after taking Thomas's explanation of the incident in Nairobi at face value.

Khimji carried on, "then he asked me if I knew you. I said yes, why are you asking me? He told me you left your car with him, because you had to go abroad. He was now in deep shit and had to get the hell out of here, before any witnesses came forward. Then he asked me to help him and said I could keep your car as payment."

"Khimji, what are you telling me? You have my car?" I asked.

"Well, I had to pay the smugglers to get him to Dar es Salaam and give him some money, in case there was any problem on the border," he replied.

"So, where is my fucking car?" I started to get seriously pissed off.

"I sold it, but I kept twenty thousand shillings *(£ 1000 at local rate)* for you". He said it, as if he was doing me a favour. Then opened his desk drawer and took out a bundle of notes.

"Kimji, is my car wanted by the police? It is registered in my name and this idiot killed a girl with it, I could also be in trouble."

"Your German friend…"

I interrupted him. "This asshole is NOT my friend. This low life prick took advantage of me, killed a girl, stole my car, and…"

"OK, OK, don't worry about any charges or problems. I spoke to a friend at the police and nobody witnessed a car accident. All papers have been changed, anyway, and the car is now out of the country."

I was speechless, and even worse, powerless. I experienced the same feeling of loss that I had had in the casino in Hamburg, and after the property deal in Lanzarote, when I had lost most of my ill-gotten gains.

"Where is that son of a bitch?" I shouted!

"He is in Dar. If you want to go over there, I will give you a contact, who knows where to find him."

Next day I sat in a plane destined for Dar es Salaam. I took a taxi into town, booked a hotel in the centre and got in touch with Khimji's contact. I waited until next evening and went to the bar where I was told I could find Thomas. There he was, sitting with some girls, smoking a cigarette and drinking some beer. I was fuming, hell bent on knocking his lights out. I approached him from behind and tapped him on his shoulder. He turned around and nearly fainted.

"What…how did you find me?"

"Listen, I want an explanation from you. I trusted you and you fucked me up big time."

"Sorry, I…."

"Never mind, sorry, let's go to my hotel and you can tell me everything."

With this in mind, I wanted to teach him a lesson he would never forget. We sat down and he started crying and lit another cigarette.

"I'm sorry, I did not know what to do. I was in a very dark place."

"When did you kill that girl?" I asked him.

"It was on the way back from the airport. It was dark and somehow I did not see her. It happened so fast. I panicked and drove back to your apartment, as I thought it was a safe place to park the car. Next day I went to Khimji, as I remembered you gave me his address."

I said nothing, only looked down at him. There he was, a broken man. He had no passport, little money and no future in this part of Africa. Suddenly, instead of beating the shit out of him, I felt sorry.

"You are very lucky I am a softy. I had plans for you, but now I feel nothing else but pity. You betrayed me, you stole my car, and you killed a young girl. In my eyes, you are a fucking useless piece of shit and deserve whatever will happen to you. The only good news for you is that I am leaving now, without going through what I had planned for you, because you are not worth the effort. I will leave it for others to punish you, which I'm sure will happen, because I will not dirty my hands on you, you useless, selfish bastard."

I left the meaning of this threat hanging in the air, for his own interpretation and for him to worry about what I said.

He looked at me as if he wanted to say something.

"Just fuck off before you regret it," I said. With this, he left. Next day I flew back to Mombasa and realised suddenly that this episode was a changing point in my life. A life I will not miss. I was now yearning for a more peaceful life.

Some months later, I heard that the Health Minister of Uganda was now driving my Mercedes Benz car.

I started to enjoy my life in Mombasa and made contacts with many expats, but many more with local people. Ashura now came every day and worked hard, inspecting stones, cutting, and polishing them and haggling with new suppliers. I had no car and lived out of town in the bush.

Hans came to visit me from time to time. One evening I suggested playing poker and the game became quite tense and fiery and the stakes got higher. At the end, well after midnight and a great deal of consumed alcohol, I had won. He did not have enough cash, so he offered me his Mini Moke as payment instead. I was mobile again.

CHAPTER 33

Settling in and embracing Africa

I had such a crazy life. How I got away with it, I don't know

Jake LaMotta

I felt comfortable in my surroundings. On many days I went to the Mombasa Beach Hotel where I joined Werner for lunch or dinner. The hotel was owned by Kenya's President Jomo Kenyatta. I often saw him during the summer months and exchanged greetings. His residence was nearby and he would come for lunch with his wife and Vice President Daniel arap Moi. There was security everywhere, but somehow it did not interfere with the tourists. As soon as the President's car was visible on the road, all cars had to stop and all passengers had to step outside, in some bizarre security ritual. I saw many times people dragged out of their cars and beaten up, if they did not obey.

With Werner's help I now had gemstone display cabinets in four hotels and spent lots of time there. Of course, during the day I promoted the gemstones to the European tourists, highlighting their amazing bargain prices. In the evening I collected the takings from the hotels.

What struck me was the number of older tourists. At first, I thought, they were just enjoying an exotic holiday after retirement, and exploring different parts of the world. However, I quickly found out that many older ladies, as well as, gentlemen had different ideas and came to Mombasa for sex. I noticed the ladies, openly kissing and touching young local men, or even boys. Many paid for these lovers to stay overnight in the hotel. The old gentlemen played the same game. I was shocked, but not surprised, that these boys and girls embraced this opportunity to make money. I started to know some of them quite well, and they realised I did not condemn or judge them. They supported their families with amounts of money they could only have dreamed of, before these tourists came to Mombasa. It was not uncommon to see young men proudly wearing large gold chains or jewellery that had been gifted to them.

I was told of an incidence, where a lady invited her lover to Switzerland and married this young man. However, because of the clash of two different cultures this marriage did not last long.

Hans and I stayed in contact and I went with him to a number of places in Kenya, where he provided eye tests for locals. However, my main sources of entertainment were the hotels around Nyali beach. There was only one night club in

Mombasa, called the 'Sunshine Club' on Kilindini Road. It was the meeting point for locals, expats, as well as sex seeking tourists. At the beginning, these girls often propositioned me, but as soon as they realised I would not be a paying client and was a resident in the town, they changed their approach and left me in peace. Many times, I sat with them, as they shared their problems with me, and from time to time, I supported them. I never considered or thought to judge them and therefore, I always had a good, friendly relationship with most of them.

I understood very quickly, Africa works very differently to Europe. My moto became, 'Do not ask questions, and go with the flow', because most times there is no logic in whatever you see, been told or experienced. Hans had the right idea to shorten any conversation. If somebody approached and started greeting him, with "How are you?" he would not even wait to hear the question, but would answer first, "Fine, thank you."

I always had to laugh when I witnessed that.

I became friends with a Member of Parliament. He invited me to his house. We had a drink and a lively conversation about Africa, its problems and future, in particular the future of Kenya. I think, he wanted to show me his wealth. His lounge was a mixture of many styles, with a throne like chair, a sign that he was a sheik or chief. Finally, during our tour of the house we entered a fully fitted kitchen, complete with two integrated gas ovens as well as a freestanding gas hob. In the middle of the tiled floor sat an old woman, whom he introduced as his mother. She was busy, plucking a chicken, sitting next to an open fire. I realised then why she did not use the ovens, because there was no gas supply in the house.

I stuck to my motto; 'Do not ask questions.'

*

One evening I drove into town. As I entered Kilindini Road, I saw a boy lying on the payment. He must have been around fourteen years old. I stopped and approached him. His face and body were covered in blood.

"What happened to you?" I asked him

"I have been robbed and beaten up:" His voice was faint and blood poured from the top of his head.

"Come, you must get to the hospital. I will take you."

"I can't, I have no money to pay for treatment," he whispered.

"Never mind, you are coming with me" I helped him into the Mini Moke and drove him to the hospital. I had to support him, as we walked in. There was nobody at the reception. I shouted, but there was no answer. I went down the corridor and opened a door, realising, I had just entered a working operating theatre. None of the staff reacted or approached me, to tell me to get out. I shouted to a staff member: "There is a badly injured boy in reception; he is losing a lot of blood. I fear for him. "

"Wait!" was the short, sharp answer.

"It is urgent, I think he could die," I pleaded.

"I said wait! Sit in reception."

Twenty minutes later, a nurse came and led us into the theatre. The boy lifted his hand from his head and the blood was still flowing, he seemed now very weak. The nurse treated him by putting only a bandage on his head. What shocked me was the partly blood stained floor, and an old, rusty drum next to the treatment stretcher, in which she just tossed the blood-drenched towels. There was no use of disinfectant or any other hygienic treatment. Finally, she demanded that I pay one hundred shillings for his treatment, which I did, but when I asked her for a receipt, she just laughed and walked away. It seemed that money was more important than the life of a small boy.

The young boy said thank you to me and after I asked him if he would be OK, he left. I never saw him again, so I do not know if he recovered.

I sat in my Mini Moke outside the hospital, unable to leave and contemplated what had just happened. Gone were the glittering lights of the posh hotels, only dim lamps tried to fight off the surrounding darkness of these depressing corridors. I noticed some poor souls sitting or lying in front of the hospital in total darkness, maybe they needed some treatment, or were waiting for some help. This was the dark side of Africa, no tourist would see. These forgotten people were the victims of widespread corruption that only enriched small elite and paid for their large houses and fancy cars. A country like Kenya, with all the riches of its abundant nature, should not allow such inequality. My occupied mind hoped for a sign of a brighter future for this beautiful country with its beautiful people. I left the hospital in an angry and downbeat mood, from seeing the other side of life.

*

Another incident where I witnessed how local people were treated happened, when one weekend Hans asked me if I would come with him, to the island of Lamu, near the border with Somalia. He had booked some eye tests for the people there.

We met just before dawn at the bus station in Mombasa and boarded the coach to Lamu. His large suitcase with frames, glasses and optical equipment was placed on the roof rack. I could see that Hans had already taken his drugs, as he was very lethargic in his conversation with me. I did not mind, as I looked forward to this eight hour journey to see other parts of Kenya.

It was a colourful mixture of local people that had boarded this clapped out vehicle. The first stop of the trip was in the town of Malindi. Some people hopped off and new passengers joined us. I was sitting at the window and fell asleep. Suddenly, I woke up, as bits and pieces fell on my head. A woman had placed her chickens on the rack above me and the feathery friends had decided to empty their basket on me. After cleaning myself, I joined in the laughter with my fellow travellers.

During the journey, we had to cross a river, but unfortunately, as we tried to drive onto a peculiar looking platform that acted as a ferry, the bus gave up the ghost. We all helped to push the bus onto the floating platform, which was connected on each side of the river by a cable. The men had to pull the cable to move the platform across to the other side, and then we had to push the bus up the embankment. I was drenched with sweat. After some mechanical repair work, we continued our journey.

Finally, we arrived that evening at the bus stop in Lamu where we hired a canoe for a short ride across to the island. Hans had booked a small guest house. Although the house was constructed of bricks, inside it was sparsely furnished, including two clapped out beds. We had a couple of beers and went to bed.

Next morning, we arrived at the small hall he had hired to treat his patients and found a long queue of locals already waiting for their eye tests. He put his reading charts onto the wall and started his tests. It was obvious to me, that he had taken drugs again. Many times I had to tell him what the patients had read off the chart so he could prescribe the correct lenses. He also sold them frames. I noticed a number of the patients walking out in a strange way, as if their vision was blurred. I saw one man nearly hitting a lamp post. I am sure Hans was not fully *compos mentis* enough to do a thorough job. I felt sorry for how they were treated, but there was no point in mentioning this to Hans.

I stuck to my motto: Don't ask any questions.

We stayed for two days in Lamu, business was brisk and the suitcase soon filled with shilling notes. On the last night, we had a heavy drinking session to cope with the heat, the noise and mosquitos at our accommodation.

Next day, we called 'our ferryman' and his canoe took us back to the mainland. We waited for the bus, which arrived two hours late. Time is not a great issue in Africa. The driver secured our case with all its money, glasses and frames on the roof rack. It was virtually the same mixture of passengers as on the way to Lamu. We were again the only white people on the bus.

"Hans, are you not worried about the case with all its money, strapped to the roof?" I asked him. "Hans!" He had fallen asleep. The drugs had taken hold of him again.

After two hours, the coach stopped at a small village near Kibusu. Some passengers got off. Hans told the driver in Swahili we would go for a drink and some food at a wooden shack near the bus stop. The driver told us to be back in twenty minutes.

It was very dark in the shop, with a limited selection of supplies.

Hans ordered the drinks in Swahili, "Tafadhali nataka bia mbili baridi sana."(Two, very cold, beers, please).

The person serving us went to an enormous fridge and brought us four bottles of warm beer. As there was no electricity in the village, the fridge was only a front. We were very tired and after the first bottle of this warm brew, we fell asleep.

I woke up and walked outside. The bus had gone! It had left with all the money and equipment. I ran back into the hut.

"Hans! I shouted!" There was no reaction for he was gone with the fairies. "Hans, the bloody bus has gone!" I screamed at him, "The case with all the money, gone!" It took a while for him to come around, before he realised what had happened.

"Let's go to the bus," he mumbled.

"There is no fucking bus, Hans, it's gone!"

He got up and opened the door. "Shit, where is the son of a bitch?"

Hans asked the shopkeeper in Swahili if he had a car.

"No, there is nobody here who has a car, but my brother, who lives in the next village, has a Land Rover. I can go and get him. It will take me half an hour to get there, if he is at home."

"OK," Hans replied. The shopkeeper got on his bike and one and a half hours later, a rusty Land Rover stopped in front of the hut.

"Jambo, bwana," he greeted us. "What can I do for you?"

Hans explained to him that we had to catch the bus that was on its way via Malindi to Mombasa. "Hakuna matatta," he replied. "I want five shilling per kilometre, until we catch the bus. Agreed?"

We had no other choice, but to agree. Off we went, chasing the bus with all our belongings. It took us over two hours until we saw a cloud of dust on the horizon, and recognised our bus.

Suddenly, our driver slowed down. "There is something wrong with the tyres," he announced and stopped the car, got out and inspected them. "I think I have to change a tyre, it looks very flat."

I got out and realised there was nothing wrong with them. I finally convinced him to drive on, as our bus disappeared into the distance. After a couple of kilometres, he stopped again. I was convinced that he had stalled the engine on purpose. Again, he got out and inspected the car. He was playing a cunning game to extract more money from us. Just before Malindi, we caught up with the bus and he dropped us at the bus station. I laughed and said to Hans,

"This cheating little bastard deserves every shilling that his tricks have earned him. Good luck to him."

We paid him his fee, which he pocketed with a broad smile. We then boarded the bus. Neither the bus driver nor we said a word. The only two white people, he had forgotten to collect, sat down, as if nothing had happened, and we arrived in Mombasa.

I stuck to my motto; 'Don't ask any questions.'

I had the opportunity to go on another business trip with Hans, experiencing another part of this astonishing country. It was from Mombasa to Nakuru, which took us a full day, but it was worth it, although the stretch of road from Nairobi to Nakura that we had to negotiate was apparently the most dangerous road in the world. I thought my driving experience between Mombasa and Nairobi was bad, but this section was hell. You only should attempt to drive and survive on this road, if you believe in God and in the power of prayer. After 190 kilometres of hard driving from Nairobi, we arrived at Lake Nakuru, which glistened in the evening sun in the most beautiful pink colour. There they were, thousands of flamingos on the move, as if on parade. I asked Hans to stop, as I wanted to lock this breathtaking image of another unforgettable moment into my heart, because my camera still lay somewhere in the bush in Tsavo.

*

The weather became extremely hot and the humidity made it very difficult to do anything. I spent most of my time in the coolness of the Mombasa Beach Hotel with Werner. I went home after darkness, opened a bottle of cold beer, jumped in the swimming pool, and afterwards sat many evenings on the veranda, as I had no air-conditioning. The heat became nearly unbearable.

There was no rain for over six months.

One day during this time, I saw our security guard talking in an agitated voice to some people. I went out and asked what the problem was. He pointed to something that looked like a black piece of rope, hanging in the tree, outside my apartment.

"Black Mamba, deadly snake. One bite, you dead," he announced.

What I thought was a rope, turned out to be one of the most poisonous snakes on the planet, which had fallen into the pool in its search for water. He had fished it out of the pool, and killed it. From that moment on, I inspected the pool every time, before I went for a swim.

*

One Sunday morning I went to the market to buy a lobster, costing twenty shillings (one pound sterling), and stopped for a drink at the hotel. I noticed a person I had not seen before. We made contact and he introduced himself as Peter, and we started to chat. It turned out; he was originally from England, but had lived for some years on the coast in Malindi, north of Mombasa. He was a friend of Steve.

"I have just come from Tanzania, and met Steve at his coffee plantation. I told him I was on my way to Mombasa for a little break and he mentioned that he met you at the Manor House and sends you his best wishes."

"Thank you, that is very kind. Steve is a very nice chap and I feel sorry for him and for all his problems and threats. I hope he will be OK. Please, send him my regards," I replied to Peter.

"Well, he mentioned to me, if I saw you to invite you to visit him."

"Wow, that is very kind of him," I replied. "So, what are your plans in Mombasa?"

"I want to have some days on the beach and explore the area. I reckon I will stay for three or four days and then head back to see Steve. If you want, you could come with me and we could spend some time with him. We also could visit some very famous parks."

"That sounds OK with me, as I now have my business set up and trust that everything is in place, as well as it can be in a place like Africa," I smiled. "Listen, if it helps you, I am happy for you to stay with me and I can introduce you to some friends."

Had I forgotten my promise to be less trusting in people I did not know? I just hope this time there would be no disappointment, as Peter had declared he was a friend of Steve.

We shook hands, and I felt another exciting episode of my life was about to begin. I had heard so much about the famous Masaai Mara and the unique wild life at the Ngorongoro crater. Moreover, driving through the Serengeti National Park, one of nature's most important landmarks on our planet, made my heart surge with excitement.

Peter and I got on well and we planned our journey to see Steve. I also spoke to my partner, Michael, asking him to keep an eye on Ashura while I was away and also look after the showcases in the hotels, and collect any money from the sales.

All was set, for another exciting chapter of my life in Africa.

CHAPTER 34

An adventure of a lifetime

Let everything happen to you, beauty and terror, just keep going, for no feeling is final

Rainer Maria Rilke

It was time to explore and experience the real Africa.

After a pleasant weekend with Peter, we took our lives in our hands, and drove again on the most dangerous road from Mombasa to Nairobi. I felt cold and reached for my jacket; the temperature at altitude around Nairobi was much lower than in Mombasa. We slept one night, in the same small B & B, outside Nairobi, where I had stayed during my previous visits, trying to obtain my trade licence. It was a nice, clean place located at the edge of the Nairobi National Park. The lady owner remembered me and greeted me warmly. We had our breakfast in beautiful sunshine in the garden, which overlooked the mountains. We said good-bye to our host, and proceeded on our route, which took us into the Maasai Mara

Game Reserve. On the way, we had our first puncture. Whilst Peter was changing the tyre, I asked him jokingly,

"Do you want me to look out for lions?"

"Don't worry about me, I am nearer the door than you and I will lock it when I'm inside," he replied laughing.

We did not see a square inch of tarmac, as we drove for miles and miles on sandy, dusty and bumpy roads, navigating potholes and other obstacles, which tested our car to the maximum. It certainly was not a trip for people with loose teeth.

We arrived at the Maasai Mara area, a preserved savannah wilderness in southwestern Kenya, which shares a border with Tanzania. Its residents include lions, cheetahs, elephants, zebras and hippos. Wildebeest traverse its plains during their annual migration. The landscape with its rolling hills is crossed by the Mara and Talek rivers. We passed the occasional tourist safari vehicle and Peter would ask the drivers, if they could point us in the direction of where they had seen any wildlife. On one occasion, we saw a pair of giraffes. Peter stopped the car and I could not resist, so I got out and walked nearer to these two impressive animals. Suddenly, they noticed me and started to run. Their elegant movements appeared as if they were running in slow motion. I ran after them for a while, but they disappeared into the bush.

"You are crazy! Thank God no lions were chasing you," Peter said.

"I have a little surprise for you. I have been in this area quite often and have befriended some Maasai. We will pass one of their villages and we can stop there. I will introduce you to some of these warriors."

After another two hours of bumpy roads, we arrived at a small settlement. The first thing I noticed was the strong smell of cattle. The Maasai live in co-existence with the wildlife and herds of cattle and goats; therefore need a lot of land. Unlike many other tribes in Kenya, the Maasai are semi-nomadic. Young, very tall, fearsome looking men greeted us. Due to the ever-increasing tourism and with it the opportunity of making good money, some of the young men spoke an interesting form of English. They greeted us, dressed in their shuka. (*Affectionately known as the "African blanket"*)

I was mesmerized by them and commented on, how beautiful the women looked, dressed in their colourful outfits with their everlasting smiles. The young man who spoke English replied,

"They are wearing big, beaded collars and each colour represents something. Red means bravery and strength, blue is the colour of the sky and rain, white shows the colour of a cow's milk, green symbolizes plants, orange and yellow means hospitality and black shows the hardships of the people."

He also mentioned that the tribe has to be aware at all times of lions attacking the cattle.

I thanked him for having us as their guests and he simply smiled at me. We spent some hours with them, during which time they invited me to have a go at their 'adumu' (jumping dance). They got a good laugh out of me.

After that, we said good-bye and drove towards our next destination, the famous Gnorongoro crater. We crossed into Tanzania and entered the Serengeti National Park. It felt, as if I had stepped into a different world. What I had only seen on the TV became reality. Wonders of the world opened up in front of me and I was in the middle of it.

We had to stop at a small lake, as we got our second puncture. During the break, I wandered around the lake and watched a bloat of hippos, unabashedly bathing in the water. With only their heads visible, their tusks looked dangerous. I realised suddenly that one of the hippos had started to swim towards me, wiggling his ears furiously, displaying his threatening mood. As I had no intention to die young, I quickly retreated.

Our next stop to repair the spare tyre again, as well as having a rest from this strenuous and exhausting trip was at a small settlement. Peter knew Abdu, the owner of the garage and we invited him for dinner at a local *'restaurant'*. The food was simple and honest, filling and full of flavour. What it missed in pleasing the eye, it made up for in its tasty and hearty goodness. In local traditions, Tanzanian style, we ate with our hands from communal dishes in the centre of the table. Peter had to translate for me, as the conversation was in Swahili. Abdu gave us some tips for our visit to the Ngorongoro crater. He also suggested that we contact his relative, a local tour guide, called Msia.

"That should save you time and money. Msia will not be treating you as tourists, just mention my name. He will advise you where to hire a car, which you will need to enter the crater and if you give him some money he also will be your guide."

Peter thanked Abdu for all his help and after some cups of chai tea, we said goodnight and went to our simple accommodation. Next morning Abdu came to see us,

"You will find Msia at the filling station, or at the Gnorongoro Lodge entrance to the crater."

We shook hands and finally said good-bye. We started on our trip towards the Ngorongoro crater. Situated in the district of northern Tanzania, it has one of the largest gatherings of elephants, lions, leopards, buffalos and rhinos. We witnessed wildebeests crossing our way and zebras traversing the plains right in front of us. In the midst of this, we experienced our third puncture, but this time we had to be very careful, as the local wildlife was never very far away.

We arrived at the petrol station near the crater and asked for Msia.

"He left for the lodge an hour ago," we were informed.

Once our spare tyre puncture was repaired, we carried on, and after a short drive met him at the lodge and introduced ourselves.

"Msia, we have just come from Abdu. He told us to get in touch with you."

"I know," he smiled, "you are Peter and a good friend of Abdu. The bush telegraph already informed me that you were coming."

"How come?" I shook my head in amazement.

Laughing loudly, Msia said, "Ha-ha, no magic, it was a driver who came from Abdu this morning, and told me that you were on your way."

"Msia, we would like to ask you, if you could organise hiring a car and would consider, being our guide for a day. Of course we will pay you."

Somehow, the smile never left Msia's face. It seemed he was happy to help us. "It's OK, the car has been reserved and I am very happy to be your guide."

Wherever I went in Africa, I noticed this smile on people's faces. It seemed to me, as if it was permanently painted on the faces, of even tribes living in harsh conditions, fighting for their existence. This showed me a side of life, many of us, in the so-called civilised world, had forgotten. It came to me like a lesson. 'You don't have to be rich to be happy'.

I loved Africa more and more.

After some formalities, we jumped into the rented Jeep, ready for this extraordinary adventure. As we approached the Ngorongoro entrance, we saw a queue of tourist cars waiting to enter.

"Not for us," Msia smiled, "you are VIP today."

After he spoke to some of his colleagues, we drove straight through, and didn't have to pay anything. However, I gave Msia some money for his friends, to say thank you for their kindness. Of course, we also had the great advantage that Msia knew the crater inside out and guided us to places where we could experience the wildlife close up. It was a good start for us, to see one of the natural wonders of the world.

"There, under the tree," his finger pointed at a pride of lions. "Look at the male lion, lying on his back, with his legs in the air. I think his belly must be full."

There was a group of four adults and three cubs, lying there, as if inviting us to stroke them. The magic carried on, as we observed herds of elephants, buffalo and giraffe. It was a most surreal, out of this world experience. I had to pinch myself, to make sure I was not dreaming.

We stayed in the crater until the sun slowly disappeared, which was nature's way of telling us to leave and drove back to Msia's village. We had a pleasant dinner and plenty of laughs, until we realised it was nighttime.

"It is very dangerous to drive now towards Arusha, I would not recommend it," he warned us. "My brother has a small house you could sleep in. Just give him some money and he will be ok."

We put our heads down, but did not have a very peaceful night, as the mosquitos and creepy crawlies had other ideas.

We thanked Msia for all his help and time he had spent with us and went on our way. We stopped in Arusha for a meal and a rest, before trying to find Steve's plantation. Thank God, Peter had been there before, as I never would have found it on my own. After some frantic searching, as there was not one human being in sight to ask, we finally found Steve's coffee plantation, tucked away near the village of Komolo, about one hundred kilometres south of Arusha.

"Hi Peter, I got your phone call when you left Mombasa, glad you found me again. Rudi, good to see you, I am happy that you two met and were able to make it," he greeted us. "Let's have some nice, relaxing days in my 'kingdom,'" he seemed very happy to receive our company.

"What's new in Mombasa, Rudi?" he asked.

"Well, there is plenty to tell, but the long and the short of story is that I let a German guy use my car. He killed a young girl in an accident, then he stole the car and did a runner to Dar. The irony is, I helped this bastard to hide from the police."

"Wow," Peter uttered. "I had no idea. Did you catch him?"

"Yes, I went to Dar es Salaam to confront him, but thought it was not worthwhile to waste my time with him. Anyway Steve, I am not sure if you know but I am now dealing in gemstones."

He shook his head.

"A bunch of low lives came to see me in Mombasa, offering me a large consignment of Tanzanite. I found out that they wanted to rob me and put me out of business. Werner lent me a couple of rifles and I went with my friends to meet them, to make sure they did not try that again," I said.

"Bloody hell! And all that happened in such a short time after you arrived in Mombasa," he said. "And I think I have problems. Come on let's forget all that shit and let us have a drink."

We sat on his veranda until midnight, while his cook prepared us a delicious meal. The view was just breath taking, overlooking the mountains. The sunset was so spectacular, and its beauty nearly made me cry, it was overwhelming. In this special moment, I forgot my crazy life, the big cars, the money and the people I had met on my life's journey. Apart from the occasional noise of some wildlife, there was no sound. One could think we were in The Garden of Eden, but the reality was quite different, as Steve explained later.

Next morning, after a large breakfast, Steve drove us through the coffee plantation.

"This year we are having such a severe drought, which I have never seen so bad, during all my life here. It looks like, I will have to let some of my staff go, as large parts of the crop will be destroyed. I really feel sorry for them, because their life is not an easy one, anyway," he explained. "There is no support from the government, so they have to fend for themselves." He turned to me," Rudi, you can see under what strain I'm living here. It is not only the drought, which worries me or looking after my people, it is also the threat from the local governor, who has an eye on my business here. He tries hard to throw me out of the country."

I could see the worries visible all over his face and felt sorry for him.

"If I have to pack up here, God only knows what will happen to my staff, my people. I know for sure, he only will employ his cronies to manage the estate and I am telling you, the plantation will go bust within months of his involvement, because he or nobody else from his tribe has the faintest idea how to run this place. Let's hope it will not come to this," he sighed heavily. "Enough of my moaning, let's enjoy ourselves, although I can't offer you any bars or night clubs within one hundred kilometres," he laughed.

We went back to his house and started a large drinking session, which only stopped when there was nothing more to drink.

Next morning, after several rounds of headache tablets and a wholesome meal, Steve said, "Rudi have you visited Kilimanjaro?"

"No," I replied.

"Well, we will drive to Moshi, a small town near the mountain and have lunch at a hotel there, so you don't forget completely what civilisation looks like," he announced.

It was nice to drive, finally on a tarmacked road again, until we arrived at the hotel restaurant in the centre of Moshi. Steve asked the waiter to give us a table at a window, so we could see the Kilimanjaro. It was another unforgettable wonder of Africa, which I took to my heart.

After our meal, Steve said to me, "We will drive to the foot of Kilimanjaro and you can walk up a bit towards the top, and feel like a mountaineer in Africa."

We walked for half an hour and then returned to the car.

Peter and I stayed one more night and the next morning, we said good-bye.

"Steve, I hope all goes well for you. I am so very sorry for the stress you are going through. I thank you for your hospitality and whenever you come to Mombasa, please be my guest."

We shook hands and left for Tanga.

Six months later, I found out that Steve was forced at gunpoint, to abandon his plantation and was given three weeks' notice to leave the country.

I felt for him deeply, kicked out like a criminal. Steve was not a paid manager, but the owner of the plantation, in which he had invested a lot of money. He had looked after 'his people' provided them with jobs and income. All his years of hard work, now counted for nothing. He had been robbed, by a rich governor, a so-called representative of the local community. It seemed to me that this sort of thing was quite common in African countries, where the white residents could be thrown out, without any legal rights or reasons. However, the same can happen to members of a different tribe. In my opinion, neither the country, nor its people will benefit from such travesty. After we left Steve, we saw evidence of what he had mentioned as the worst drought he had ever experienced. During a large stretch on our way back to Mombasa, we realised the sky was full of vultures and a smell of decay was in the air. We saw hundreds of these birds feasting on the cadavers of cattle that had died on its dry, grassless grounds. It was a devastating picture to witness.

I said to Peter, "I would like to stop one more night in a special hotel I know in Tanga, run by a lovely Greek lady. The food and hospitality was always good, with no fuss and very relaxed and fun. Let us hope she is still there. Times are changing in Africa," I said, fearing the worst.

When I entered the hotel, it felt odd and not the same. Gone was the cosiness of the reception and the staff were different. The homely atmosphere had gone. When I approached the reception, there were no greetings of 'Can I help you?' I asked the man behind the desk,

"Could I have a word with the owner? I met her last time I stayed here and I want to say hello."

"She has gone," was the short answer. "Do you need a room?"

"No thank you." I turned around and did not ask any further questions, because deep down, I knew the answer.

We drove to the border and took the coast road to Mombasa, where Peter carried on to his place in Malindi.

"Rudi, it was a pleasant and eventful trip. Let's keep in touch, maybe you will come and visit me in Malindi, you are always welcome."

*

After returning from the trip, I went home and straight to bed, as I was still tired from the journey. In the middle of the night, I was woken by a loud noise. It took me a while to realise that it was rain hammering down on my corrugated iron roof. I opened my veranda door and ran out, dancing in the first rain after six months. Never mind any black mambas. I heard some more noise from other places, as people enjoyed this long awaited relief from the drought. This night was full of happiness and hope.

I settled back in, concentrated on my business and spent a lot of time in the different hotels, where I had my showcases, selling and keeping an eye on my gemstones. I also joined Werner's air pistol shooting club, where we had some memorable evenings, talking about our upbringing and life in Hamburg. We both shared the same reasons, about why we left because we felt trapped and needed to see and experience the world.

Then my first Christmas arrived in Africa. It was one of the most bizarre experiences. I invited some local friends and neighbours, living in the nearby village for a Christmas Eve celebration, bearing in mind; it was 32 degrees in the evening. To be festive, I tried to put some candles on a small tree and on our bar, but they immediately melted. Earlier, I had driven into Mombasa and bought some large blocks of ice, which I placed in a rubber dingy. That would sort the cool drinks out for the night, I thought.

We prepared a large piece of mutton, which my local friends started to barbeque on an open fire pit. With all their expertise, they prepared a delicious meal for us, although the meat was quite chewable.

After our festive meal and some more fizzy wine, gin, Bacardi and local brews, some of us decided to go for a swim in our pool. I told our local neighbours about the Black Mamba we fished out of the pool and then no one wanted to go for a dip. It became a memorable night in which Europeans and Africans danced and got drunk, until the sun showed its face. Finally, the locals walked back to their village, whilst Urs drove the others back into Mombasa.

Next morning I woke up with an earth-shattering hangover. As I had no air-conditioning, I wanted to jump in the pool. I could not believe my eyes. On our outside bar, I noticed a group of monkeys, sitting on some chairs, lying on the bar and rolling in the grass. Beer and gin bottles were scattered all over the place. They saw me and made their getaway. Some of them even took a beer bottle with them, whilst others fled in an unstable zigzag, obviously drunk. I saw this group many times around my apartment, but never like this. I made a note for the future, to ask the gardener to always clear the bar after a party.

*

From 1974, Kenya became quite unsettled or even dangerous, as the President of Uganda, also known as the "Butcher of Uganda," had been expelling thousands of Indian residents since 1972. Most of them were business people. The Ugandan economy collapsed and many locals became unemployed and fled to Kenya. They were destitute and resorted to begging, violence and robbery. Consequently, the crime rate increased dramatically in Nairobi, and started to spill over into Mombasa. One of their main targets was tourists. In the past I had never locked my door, as I lived away from the city that now changed as I learned of the increase in mugging and threats. Somehow, the beauty of this place started to become tarnished and the peace disturbed.

One morning I woke up and felt very ill. I had problems getting out of my bed. I was finally able to put my feet on the ground, but collapsed in a heap on the floor, I could not move. It was as if I had touched a high voltage cable with sweaty hands and landed on my bottom. Not realising what had hit me, I just made it to the toilet, as vomiting and diarrhoea overcame me. I was shaking with chills and an almighty headache hammered my brain. I had a very high fever. Intense muscle aches and tiredness took hold of me. I became nauseous and I had no recollection of how I got back to bed.

I had contracted MALARIA.

I slipped in and out of consciousness and could not distinguish between day and night. I remember once, crawling to the toilet, which took me maybe fifteen to twenty minutes. Then I looked into the mirror and I did not recognise my yellow face, with sunken cheeks and yellow eyes. I looked like death.

Hans, who found me after six days because he had not heard from me, told me I had had a most severe attack of malaria and if he had not have found me, I might have died.

"Rudi, you might not be out of the woods yet. I suggest you fly back to Switzerland, see a tropical specialist who should tell you exactly how bad it is and what to do and have a rest before you come back. OK?"

"OK," I whispered.

(The sixth intervention of my guardian angel.)

He organised my ticket and I flew to Zürich. The doctor told me that it was touch and go for me to survive, as my weight had fallen to fifty kilos. The specialist told me; I had one of the most dangerous types of malaria, called Plasmodium falciparum. It was touch and go. I looked like a skeleton. I stayed with friends for some weeks, before I got my strength back and returned to Mombasa.

Hans picked me up from the airport and dropped a bombshell.

"Rudi, I am leaving Mombasa, I don't feel safe anymore. There is more and more crime. The first killing has taken place in the 'Sunshine' night club on Kilindini Road," he paused "I have asked my company to transfer me to Nairobi and they have accepted my request. I am leaving next week and I hope you will come and visit me, as I will have a nice house with garden."

"I will miss you. We had some crazy times here, but I certainly will come to see you," I replied.

Little did he know what was waiting for him in Nairobi.

When I visited him a couple of months later he was not the same person I knew. He was nervous and had lost weight. We went to his house and I met his wife and child.

"Hans, what is going on? You are not yourself, tell me what's happened!"

"Rudi, you remember, I told you I was transferred and took over the optician shop in the centre near the Stanley Hotel in a row with other shops."

He had to stop. I could see his memories hurt him.

"Next to me was a souvenir shop run by an Indian couple. We became good friends and we looked after each other. On Friday morning I went to open my shop and noticed they were not there. Then I realised their front door was open. I shouted a greeting and as I got no answer went inside." He started crying.

"There in front of me, in a pool of blood lay their bodies, killed, hacked by a machete. I could not move. These pictures still haunt me. I called the police, gave my statement and only went back to my shop, after a week's break."

He was breathing heavily. His tears were now flowing freely.

"These pictures still haunt me," he cried.

There was nothing I could say to comfort him. He was depressed, defeated, he had a young family and therefore no choice, but to carry on, even if it hurt deeply.

I spent another day with him and we said goodbye. I didn't see the man who had brought me to Africa for a long time and I wasn't able to help him deal with his demons.

On my drive back to Mombasa I tried to analyse the situation and the impact that Hans's experience had on me. It shook me and made me think, will I stay?

I was now back in my apartment and contemplating my life here. It felt as if some dark clouds had gathered over the beauty of living here. Was it time to leave this beautiful country? I tried to weigh up my doubts against the positives. I was only in my twenties, still young enough to explore the world, to find my fortune somewhere else. My free spirit, my appetite for new adventures, started slowly moving up the ladder. Let me sleep on it, was what my inner voice was telling me.

Next morning I walked around in the garden. I looked over the blue ocean and waved to the locals passing by. I thought I'm still young; the word is my oyster. Who knows what I can do next and where I will end up.

Next day I had lunch with Werner. "Where have you been? Nobody has seen you for weeks. Is everything OK?" he asked.

I explained to him that I had contracted malaria and had not been able to leave my apartment or contact anybody.

"If my friend Hans had not found me after six days, I think I would have had celebrated my last birthday already."

I also told him that Hans had organised for me to fly to Zürich and see a doctor.

"You still look a bit under the weather. Are you OK now?"

"Yes, thank you, I'm getting my strength back."

"Come on, let's have a drink of the best medicine for malaria," he smiled.

We finished a number of gin and tonics and I drove home. I was still tired and exhausted and low on any motivation.

*

A few months later, it was a beautiful, sunny day, as it was every other day, but this day became very special. I went for a swim and went back inside the apartment for a bite to eat. I glanced through my window and saw two young ladies lying on sunbeds by the pool. I thought maybe they were friends or relatives of the landlord. One of them got up and walked towards the apartments. I quickly ran outside the back door as she came round the corner. I was mesmerized by this most attractive lady. I had no idea what had happened to me, but my heart started pounding.

I thought I might go back out to the pool and maybe get to know the ladies more. I went out and moved a sunbed nearer to theirs. The other lady looked younger so I thought it might be her sister. After a few minutes later the lady came back out, carrying beers in a bag. She lay on her sunbed and smiled at me.

"Have you got a beer for me?" were my first words to her. That must have been the most pathetic or most successful chat-up line ever.

She turned around and said, "YES"……… this was a pivotal moment in my life and helped make my decision.

That answer changed my life forever!

ACKNOWLEDGEMENTS

I would like to thank my wife, for putting up with my lack of patience and occasional outbursts, and saving me from drifting onto the rocks of destruction. She saw in me what nobody else did and believed in me during anxiety, stress and hard times.

I would like to thank both my wife and my good friends for their support in helping me to translate my English into correct readable grammar. Ted Goodliffe, through whom I detected the secret and the abundant use of commas, and Stefan Kokotka for helping me streamline my thoughts.

Also would like to say thanks to all our close family for their encouragement and support.

A massive thank you to Joe Topliffe, for helping me get the book published.

Printed in Great Britain
by Amazon

66193584R00173